GARDENING ON
THE COAST

GARDENING

ON THE COAST

by

CHRISTINE KELWAY

DAVID & CHARLES : NEWTON ABBOT

ISBN 0 7153 4993 7

Distributed in USA by
Transatlantic Arts New York

Set in 11/13 Baskerville
and printed in Great Britain
by Clarke, Doble & Brendon Limited
for David & Charles (Publishers) Limited
South Devon House Newton Abbot Devon

CONTENTS

LIST OF ILLUSTRATIONS

7

List of Illustrations (continued)

ACKNOWLEDGEMENTS

I am most grateful to the following for supplying photographs :
Mr Neil Treseder, Mr Bishop, Mr Elcock, Mrs Marny Macintosh,
Mrs Bickford Smith and Major Wynn Werninck

INTRODUCTION

IT is eight years now since I wrote *Seaside Gardening*, and during that time I have received many requests from readers for more about 'Gardening on the Coast'. This then is the title of my new book.

Years of gardening on the coast, with its disappointments and its thrills, have in no way diminished for me the pleasure and excitement of this particular form of gardening, so different from gardening inland. It has lost none of its original attraction, and our garden, with its windbreaks of modern artificial screens and living shelter of salt-resistant plants, has amply repaid the labour we have put into it, and enables me to write of tender plants which will grow by the sea when given shelter.

Readers of my earlier book have asked me to tell them how and when to prune their seaside shrubs, and this I have now done. Many also wanted to know of vegetables in seaside conditions and, since housing-estates are springing up like mushrooms around our coasts, frequent reference has been made to the small modern garden and what to grow in the mini-plot.

A very special bond unites those of us who garden by the sea, as I found when *Seaside Gardening* was published. It has brought me many friends both in this country and from many parts of the world, to whom I would like to say 'thank you' for useful information under climatic conditions vastly different from our own, but who all tell how best to defeat those enemies of seaside gardening—Wind, Salt and Sand.

Cornwall, 1970 Christine Kelway

9

I

WIND, SALT AND SAND

THERE is an almost perpetual battle being waged between the sea on the one hand and living plants on the other. Most coastal districts are ravaged by salt-laden gales at intervals from mid-October to mid-April, and also at other times of the year when storms blow up unexpectedly, blackening and scorching seaside plants and stunting their growth. Such gales tend to be more frequent in autumn and winter but may occur at any time, and a rapidly falling or rising glass is always a danger signal.

The effect of winds off the sea cannot be over-estimated. Cruel gales, carrying salt, have an evil effect on trees and shrubs and, with some few exceptions, on plant life generally. Scorch marks and blackening of the edges of leaves are often attributed to fungus or disease, when, in fact, high winds are to blame. Violent wind in exposed inland situations can be very destructive but salt-laden winds straight off the sea, their force unbroken by buildings, trees or the contour of the land, do incalculable harm. I have known plants that have taken years to reach maturity to be killed outright by a particularly vicious gale. It is a hazard all seaside gardeners must face.

Salt is carried in the spray and when, in its turn, this is caught up by the wind, it is deposited over the land for a con-

11

siderable distance, frequently several hundreds of yards, and
in specially violent storms even further. It settles on everything
within reach, coating windows and cars left in the open with
a film of sticky, salty moisture which is difficult to remove and
encrusts the leaves of plants with damaging effect. Plants that
do withstand it, grow in spite of it and not because they like
it. They cannot make use of the salt, and unless rain comes to
wash it off they will soon die. Should a period of fine, dry
weather follow a severe storm, then a hosing-down of trees
and shrubs will be beneficial.

Salt is enemy enough, but not enough notice is taken of the
evil effects of sand, picked up off the beach or nearby sand
dunes. Marram grass and sea lyme grass are the best stabilisers
for shifting sand. Shore gardens are the worse sufferers, and
again the wind is at the root of the trouble. It uses the sand
to blast and chisel the plants so that those which have lost
their leaves to salt now lose their stems to sand. Thick ground
cover is most valuable in beach gardens : plants which grow
dense enough to prevent the wind picking up the sand and
burying any plantings you have made. In the south and west,
it is worth trying the Hottentot-Fig, *Mesembryanthemum
edule*, and further north *Hypericum calycinum*, Rose of
Sharon, which looks miserable in winter but usually recovers
with the spring.

Under relatively calm conditions, sea air is balmy and the
gales that blow up with such frightening force are hard to
imagine in days of halcyon calm. Plants as well as humans
revel in it, but once an angry sea starts to play rough it brings
into force its two deadly allies, SALT and SAND, so that I have
sometimes felt that the title of this book should have been
'Wind, Salt and Sand versus Living Plants'.

The chief problem of gardening near the sea is to find enough
trees and shrubs to withstand the full blast off the sea. Shelter
is everything, and it is not possible to make a garden worth

the name without it. Great gardens by the sea are rare and
have only been accomplished by the tenacity and perseverance
of man. Tresco in the Isles of Scilly, the Isle of Gigha and
Brodick on the west coast of Scotland, and Inverewe in remote
Wester Ross, are outstanding examples. I find it scarcely possible now to envisage the lovely garden of Inverewe, visited
today by thousands of visitors from all over the world, as once
a mass of red Torridian sandstone and blasted by vicious
south-westerly gales. A hundred years ago it was devoid of
all vegetation apart from stunted heather and still shorter crow-
berry. There was nothing approaching decent soil, and in the
garden's early stages of development soil had to be brought
in creels to provide beds for plants. Such industry and perseverance in the face of the exposed position of the garden and
the constant likelihood of its being soused with salt have been
wonderfully and deservedly rewarded.

In making new gardens on the coast the first requisite is to
establish some sort of screen between the sea and the garden.
It could be artificial or a living windbreak. In the first instance
an artificial windbreak will help one of living material to
establish itself. Once a rampart of vegetation has been im-
posed between sea and garden the rest becomes comparatively
easy, for the choice of ornamental trees and shrubs that will
grow in close proximity to the sea, if given protection, is almost
unlimited. The climatic influence that sea masses have upon
temperature, and the humidity which is imparted to the atmosphere, are highly favourable to the cultivation of some of
the most beautiful ornamental species from other countries
than our own. On western and southern coasts, which owe
much to the kindly influence of the warm Gulf Stream and
where vegetation in many sheltered places is almost subtropical, plants coming from Australasia, Chile, Japan, China
or Southern Europe grow perfectly happily. The south coast
is drier than the west but it has the best light.

DIFFERENCES BETWEEN THE WESTERN AND EASTERN SEABOARDS

These differences are most marked; indeed, visitors to the
south-west, seeing all manner of exotic plants luxuriating in
the open, often imagine that gardening here requires no special
skills or effort. They should spend a few days when gales are
at their worst and gardens without shelter are raked and tor-
mented by high winds off the sea. Winds coming in off the
Atlantic are frequently extremely violent, uprooting trees and
removing shrubs and plants from their positions in the garden,
so that it seems as if a tornado had passed that way, but at
least they do not have the bite of the cold north-easters which
are so damaging to young growth on the east coast of Britain
early in the year. On eastern seaboards conditions are far
colder, with drying, biting winds sweeping in off the cold North
Sea for many weeks during spring and early summer so that
planting is delayed. But while the plantsman on the east coast
has planted stock that can hold its own in colder conditions,
many a garden in the west is filled with delicate, tender plants
that die when subjected to more than a few degrees of frost.
Thus any specially severe winter takes heavy toll. Trees and
shrubs on the easterly seaboard develop hard growth and there
is less moisture to freeze, while in the west the rapid growth
they make during mild autumns can be very severely checked
by rough weather early in the year.

A great deal of planting takes place in late spring in
southern and western districts after winter gales have spent
themselves, but in East Anglia it is best to plant all hardy
plants, except evergreens, in the autumn. Spring is far too
dry in most areas. The main snag is that soil often becomes
very dry indeed after mid-April, and this condition is accen-
tuated on parts of the east coast of England where there are

large areas of wind-blown sand. In these districts, and also in western coastal districts where spring planting is carried out, the use of moistened peat with the addition of a small quantity of bonemeal greatly helps plantings to get established. Dry soil should be raked around the plant to preserve moisture and a further mulch of rotted manure, garden compost, or bracken will help plantings through a long rainless period. For my part, I like to build up these mulches year after year and to feed the plants through the mulch.

Plants in containers from garden centres are most useful for this sort of late spring or early summer planting, though it cannot be stressed too often that the plant in its pot or container should be well watered before planting, and the hole should have been previously prepared and great care should be taken not to disturb the roots in any way. Make the hole large enough to take plant and soil and lift them out of the container with as little disturbance as possible. Any spreading out of the roots may result in the death of the plant. Gardeners often remind me that by spring or early summer the best plants are gone and this may well be so, since planting time for inland gardeners is traditionally the autumn. We gardeners in exposed coastal localities who do not wish to subject our plants to winter's gales, may therefore be wise to collect our plants in the autumn, leaving them in their containers in a cold frame or sheltered place in our gardens for the winter.

Trees and shrubs for seaside gardens can be very roughly divided into two main groups. Group 1 will contain the wind- and salt-tolerant ones which form the essential defence for the garden. Look for these among those specially adapted by Nature to withstand seaside conditions without injury, and among those with a maritime inheritance, whose ancestors adapted themselves to coastal environment in other parts of the world.

NATURE'S PROTECTIVE ARMOUR AGAINST WIND, SAND AND SALT

1 Grey-foliaged plants do particularly well on the coast because the surface of their leaves is covered with a minute forest of hairs. The salt crystals cannot reach the leaf's surface but only the tips of the hairs, so that rain causes the salt crystals to drop to the ground. This tomentum, as it is called, covers in a few cases both the top and the under-surface of the leaves. Very many shrubs that come to us from New Zealand are examples. In some cases the upper surface may be shiny while the under-surface is hairy.

2 High gloss is a protective armour adopted by some plants. It is a film that prevents the leaves from absorbing the salt crystals deposited on them and sand cannot find a home. Eg, *Euonymus japonicus, Pittosporum tobira* and *Coprosma retusa.*

3 In a few cases Nature has allowed plants to dispense altogether with leaves in their normally accepted form. Instead, they form tough shoots that are better able to withstand high winds and salt-spray. Eg, *Spartium junceum.*

4 The leaves of some plants develop a specially tough skin or epidermis. This is most marked in shrubs such as the shrubby Hebes (veronicas). And besides the doubling of the epidermis, the hebes use another device to protect their growing points. An effective arrangement of the leaves allows the bud to develop behind successive pairs of leaves. This protection of the buds is important, since many plants are unable to grow on after storm-damage because the leading growth has been killed.

5 Some shrubs exude a sticky gum on the leaf surface, eg, *Escallonia macrantha.* The gum distinguishes this escallonia from others whose leaves do not possess it and which do not therefore make good protective hedges close to the sea, though

Page 17: Broom and Spanish Gorse in the author's garden

Page 18: Blue sea and golden gorse on the North Cornish coast

they are excellent for seaside gardens with some shelter from direct sea-wind.

6 In exposed situations many shrubs become more and more stunted, and what in sheltered places would normally be a free-growing bush becomes an abnormally-shaped hummock. Eg, the Spanish Gorse, *Genista hispanica*, will make a rounded shape reminiscent of a hedgehog when planted in extreme exposure.

These, then, are some of the tricks and devices adopted by Nature to protect her plants from wind and salt and to allow them to grow naturally by the sea.

In Group 2 will be the more tender and ornamental species which benefit from the microclimate created within the garden. This will be many degrees warmer than the temperature outside and free from the devastating effects of salt carried by the wind and sand-blast.

THE MICROCLIMATE OF A GARDEN

The microclimate of a garden is its own particular and individual climate, a special adaptation of the general climate of the district. Though the general climate is beyond man's manipulation, being largely determined by latitude, height above sea-level and position relative to land or sea masses, since the sea retains its heat for longer than the land, the microclimate of a garden can be contrived by the ingenuity and cunning of its owner.

Nowhere is a study of the microclimate more rewarding than in a garden by the sea. First and foremost, plants need protection from the worst winds and it must be realised that if you boast a fine view of the sea, the sea can also see you and your garden. Once a garden is made there is no difficulty in discovering where the gales strike, but this bitter experience of plants browned and scorched or even killed outright need

B

not occur if sufficient attention is paid to the direction of prevailing winds at the outset. Trees in the immediate vicinity
are a clear indication from which direction the worst winds
come, and their shorn and cruelly twisted branches tell a sad
tale that should not be disregarded.

Plant only the toughest in their path and avoid the desicca-
tion of drying winds that destroy plants ill-equipped to bear
it. Pay attention, too, to the bitter north-easters should they
strike your garden, for once they arrive from this quarter they
tend to stay a very long time. Artificial screening will remove
any danger from sand, for this is dropped by the wind as soon
as it encounters opposition, but unfortunately salt is not so
easily deterred. Look for the worst trouble within 500 yards
of the sea.

No two gardens have identical problems. One may be at
sea level adjoining a sandy beach, while its more fortunate
neighbour is up on a rocky escarpment where the lash of the
waves and those two abhorred allies, salt and sand, cannot
reach. The one on the rocky shelf has all the advantages. The
sea, lashing at the cliff beneath, expends its energies against the
cliff-face and the limited amount of salt spray which drifts
over the garden above can be contained by close planting of
the most salt-tolerant plants.

Far the most difficult and the one presenting the greater
challenge to the would-be gardener is the small garden down
at sea level, with nothing between it and the battering of wind,
salt and sand. On a beautiful summer's day the situation
appears ideal and many a newcomer to seaside life has been
beguiled into building his home on a small patch of land such
as this. He cannot know of the bleak winter days when it is
nigh impossible to open his door on the sea's side, and the
small beginnings he has made in his garden during the summer
months are completely wrecked. No wonder he is discouraged
and gives up what he considers an unequal contest against the

elements. The results we know—a sandy patch of scrubby, unkempt ground with here and there a shrub waving in the wind. It is these gardens that cry out for some sort of artificial screening at the beginning, and many precious years will be lost without it. Trial and error can be devilish expensive as well as time-wasting. (See Chapter 2.)

If you think I have painted too gloomy a picture, the object has been to emphasise the absolute necessity of giving young plants shelter at the start. In exposed seaside conditions it is almost impossible to get them established without it, since it is in infancy that they are most vulnerable. The persistent gardener, however, is not easily discouraged and continues to discover which plants best stand exposure in his own particular district, planting them small and closer together than is normally done inland.

2

ARTIFICIAL AND
LIVING WINDBREAKS

THERE are several ways of approaching the problem of providing shelter for seaside gardens. The shelter can be temporary or more or less permanent, manufactured or of living material, and often the first is used simply to allow the second to get established.

ARTIFICIAL SCREENING

This can be of non-living material such as coir-netting, hazel wattles, chestnut or similar wooden fencing, lath screens or even fine-meshed wire-netting. Their advantage is that they can be erected at once and there is no waiting for the living windbreak to get established, an invaluable asset in newly-made gardens. Also they do not occupy so much space as hedges, and when we had recently to remove a dying escallonia hedge and erected in its place a screen of lath-fencing we were amazed at the amount of extra garden space it gave.

Coir-netting has a permeability of 50 per cent and is a very efficient wind-sifter. Hazel wattles are good but have a comparatively short life. Chestnut paling with an open lattice top is often used in urban gardens and has an effect similar to that of an earth-filled wall topped with shrubs. Double wire-netting of $\frac{1}{2}$in mesh has 75 per cent permeability.

A great deal of research has been carried out in recent years to find the most suitable artificial wind-shelter for crops. The Ministry of Agriculture has this to say :

'Experiments were made with solid straw bales, 50 per cent permeable lath-fencing and double thicknesses of $\frac{1}{2}$in wire-netting shelters. All were 3ft high and were arranged in 24ft squares. Previous experiments had shown that the maximum protection from wind was provided in the area between the shelter and a distance eight times the height of the shelter and to leeward of it, and that squares of this size and height were expected to give the maximum shelter. Among the crops com-pared, anemones, dwarf beans, lettuce and potatoes produced heavier, earlier or better quality products when sheltered by the semi-permeable lath-fencing. Wire-netting gave some slight protection, but only at the exposed centre was the solid barrier of value.'

Different types of obstacles can have surprising effects on wind and it is now well known that a solid wall affords little or no protection other than to plants immediately underneath it. The wind curls back on the leeward side and causes such turbulence that plants are worse off than without any shelter at all. Semi-permeable lath fencing, on the other hand, has now been established as the ideal screen.

LATH FENCING

Two things to bear in mind are the height and the density of the screen. The *density* is measured by the ratio of aperture to solid and is best in the ratio about 40 : 60. This is well illus-trated on page 45 by fencing made of 1in wide vertical laths set 1in apart, with additional larger upright posts and cross-members and bracing pieces. These screens are available in the following sizes: 10ft × 4ft, 10ft × 3ft, 10ft × 2ft, 5ft × 4ft, 5ft × 3ft, 5ft ×2ft. The sections are assembled with galvanised nails and the timber, impregnated with Tanalith, is very durable. If the windbreak is more solid than this it will tend to produce more air turbulence on the lee side and such disturbed winds do more damage than a direct horizontal wind. If, on the other hand, the windbreak is more open the force of the wind is less effectively reduced and damage can be considerable.

The *height* of such windbreaks has a direct bearing on the area of ground which will be sheltered, and although the force of the wind is reduced for a distance of up to twenty times the height of the screen, the area best sheltered is equivalent only to a distance eight times the height of the screen on the lee side. Thus a 4ft semi-permeable windbreak provides good shelter up to 32ft on its lee side, after which the protection diminishes until at 80ft the shelter ceases. For small gardens these screens are excellent in giving immediate shelter and occupying little space, but many people prefer to regard them only as a means of providing a good start for a permanent, living windbreak.

LIVING WINDBREAKS

Because shelter is the very backbone of all successful gardens subjected to direct sea winds on the coast, it seems appropriate to begin with those trees, regrettably few it is true, that have proved best able to withstand the storms and salt-laden gales which are the bane of every seaside gardener.

Where there is room for their wide spread, such trees, fronted with strong-growing evergreen shrubs, will provide the necessary protection for a very wide range of ornamental flowering shrubs that delight in the comparatively frost-free conditions they find near the sea. And, given such a shelter belt, a vast number of unusual and tender plants may be attempted with every anticipation of success.

Stand for a few minutes on some exposed cliff-top in the teeth of an on-shore gale, and then as you thankfully return to the shelter of a nearby clump of trees you will realise that the temperature is several degrees warmer than on the exposed headland, and appreciate why plants, like humans, do not endure with pleasure the ceaseless wear and tear of gale-force winds.

Only a few trees are able to withstand strong, salt-laden winds off the sea and many which make excellent windbreaks inland are a waste of time and money on the coast. So a few words of warning about plants used as windbreaks in inland situations. Beech and hornbeam can be quite useless on exposed coasts, common yew is badly damaged by salt, the oval-leaved privet becomes almost defoliated, and laurels very bedraggled. The much advertised *Cupressocyparis leylandii* frequently appears to lean after several years and does not stand up well to the direct salt-laden gales for which it is often recommended. When planted as a first line of defence this splendid fast-growing tree gets badly scorched and loses its top. It is better for the second row.

Though deciduous, leaf-losing trees are useful for sifting the wind and reducing its force, the evergreens are by far the most valuable. Even so, in situations of really violent exposure, such as on the north-east coast of Britain or in the northern isles, where there are vast tracts of gale-swept land, a dense belt of deciduous trees does help to allow a row of conifers to establish itself.

For his first line of defence the planter will obviously select trees which make dense and rapid growth in his own soil and situation. A look at those growing well in his immediate vicinity will be helpful, since few nurserymen have the audacity to put themselves within reach of the sea's disturbing influence, and there is no guarantee that trees which flourish ten or fifteen miles inland will do as well on the coast.

The width of the shelter belt will depend on the type of tree being planted. There should be more rows of deciduous than of evergreen since they must provide shelter during the winter. Two rows of evergreens should be sufficient; too many will present the solid barrier we wish to avoid at all costs. Since many trees, such as the pines, lose their lower branches with age, it is useful to plant a shrub like *Elaeagnus glabra* at the start on the sea side of the pines. This will send out climbing shoots, which will have clambered up the lowest branches by the time they are needed. The box thorn, *Lycium chinense*, is also good in this position. It flourishes on the top of cliffs in Yorkshire right in the teeth of the gales.

PLANTING

There are various problems in connection with the seaside planting of living windbreaks to be considered :

1 Preparation of the soil
2 Planting seasons
3 After care

A thorough preparation of the ground is essential and partticularly is this true for trees and shrubs which are planted as a first line of defence. Because of the difficulties they are bound to have to face, everything possible should be done to give young trees a good start and to encourage them to make robust and rapid growth so that when they rise above the artificial shelter they are capable of withstanding the elements.

When choosing young trees from a nursery, ask for those which have been transplanted from the seed bed the previous year, as these should have strong, fibrous roots. Only the strongest should be chosen, for a weak one in the nursery will seem even weaker when planted out.

Holes should be wide and deep enough to contain easily all the roots, and a stake should be put in before the plant so as not to damage the roots. If there is good soil available, sift some over the roots, and give the young tree a shake to make certain it gets down to them. Tread firmly, taking care to leave the main stem in an upright position.

As a general rule, it is possible to plant deciduous trees and shrubs at any time from early October to the end of February. On the east coast, it may be advisable to plant in late winter or very early spring. Evergreens should not be transplanted until late in the spring, or even in early summer if watering can be carried out, a mulch spread around the roots and the foliage syringed after a salty gale. After-care consists of keeping the young plants free of the weeds which compete for nourishment and moisture. If there is a drought, it will be necessary to water the plants or they may die.

Trees able to withstand salt-laden winds from the sea

Acer pseudoplatanus	The common sycamore. A good wind-sifter for inhospitable coasts and the tree most often seen in the northern isles.
Crataegus oxycantha	The common hawthorn. Will not grow above the height of a shrub but is worth planting.
Cupressus macrocarpa	Gets scorched by salt on the sea side but many a garden in the south and west is grateful for its shelter.
Cupressus mac. lutea	The golden cupressus is even more wind-tolerant than the green type.

Fraxinus excelsior	Ash is one of the hardiest deciduous trees for planting in the teeth of gales. It succeeds on heavy soils but not on chalk.
Olearia traversii	Stands wind and salt but is not frost-hardy.
Picea sitchensis	The lovely blue-green Sitka spruce from near Arctic regions. Fast growing, and good in cold northerly districts.
Pinus contorta	The Beach pine. A native of British Columbia and Alaska. Grows well on the north coast of Scotland.
Pinus latifolia	The Lodgepole pine. An ugly pine standing up to salty gales in the north.
Pinus nigra austriaca	The Austrian pine. Frost-hardy and can be recommended for every coast. Good on chalk.
Pinus calabrica	The Corsican pine. Slightly less hardy than the Austrian. Grows very fast on poor soils. Liable to blow in violent gales.
Pinus mugo	The mountain pine from the Tyrol. A dwarf bushy pine which will grow with its feet in salt water.
Pinus muricata	The Bishop pine. A handsome pine for the milder coasts and used in the Channel Isles, supposedly more salt-tolerant than *P. radiata*.
Pinus pinaster	The maritime pine. Excellent in the south and for sandy soils. Grows well at Bournemouth. Rather slow-growing.

Pinus radiata	The Monterey pine. Very fast-growing. A tree of outstanding beauty for the milder coasts. Easy from seed, seedlings will rapidly make sturdy plants.
Populus alba	The white poplar. Its grey leaves with white underfelt are attractive in the wind. A useful suckerer for exposed positions.
Populus robusta	A very vigorous deciduous tree for exposed coasts.
Populus serotina	Black Italian poplar. Late into leaf and so escapes the worst of spring gales.
Quercus Ilex	The evergreen, or holm oak. Very tough and will grow almost to the shore. Slow-growing and should be planted small.
Salix alba	The white willow. Will grow on any coast.
Salix caprea	The goat willow. Very hardy, and good on all coasts.
Sorbus aria	The whitebeam. Good for limy soils.
Sorbus intermedia	Swedish whitebeam. Distinguished from *S. aria* by the dull grey, not white, felt under the leaf.
Ulmus carpinifolia Cornubiensis	The Cornish elm. One of the most salt tolerant of deciduous trees.
Ulmus carpinifolia sarniensis	The Guernsey elm.
Ulmus glabra	Wych elm. Stands full exposure even on the coldest coasts but is unsuited for any but the largest gardens.

In many gardens close to the sea, as in shore or cliff gardens, space is too limited to permit the planting of trees as shelter. Reliance, instead, must be placed on shrubs able to put up with the battering of wind, salt and sand. Only a few will survive when fully exposed, and even some of these cannot withstand very low temperatures and are not frost-hardy. In normal winters, however, they will come through unharmed. A few, possessing no particular beauty of their own, are invaluable for protecting more worthwhile shrubs.

Shrubs for Shelter

Arundinaria japonica

Bamboo. Grows up to 8ft and is excellent for filtering wind. Easily increased by detaching individual rooted bamboos and laying them full length horizontally into 6in deep trenches in May. Shoots quickly rise from each joint, producing required shelter. A mass of this bamboo forms a wind shelter at Carae, on the west coast of Scotland. Bamboo also makes a very soundproof windbreak.

Atriplex halimus

The Tree Purslane makes quick shelter on any coast. It rarely tops 5ft but this grey-leaved shrub is very wind-tolerant and one of the best semi-evergreen shrubs for dry soils, even pure sand.

Aucuba japonica

A good seaside shrub of leathery glossy leaves, as tolerant of salt as of sooty deposits in towns. For red berries, both male and female plants should be grown.

Baccharis halimifolia

A useful hardy evergreen for

	exposed seaside planting, with a stiff upright habit.
Baccharis patagonica	Very similar to the above.
Bupleurum fruticosum	An evergreen bush of blue-green leaves and umbels of small dull yellow flowers. A good wind-stopper for dry, sandy shore gardens.
Berberis stenophylla	Makes a useful salt-resistant hedge, even on top of a wall. Trim after flowering.
Cistus crispus	Will grow right at the sea's edge. A low bush of crinkled grey-green leaves and magenta-pink saucer flowers.
Cistus laurifolius	A very wind- and salt-tolerant cistus with leathery green leaves and white saucer flowers opening from bright red buds.
Elaeagnus glabra	A handsome tall shrub of oval, bronze-backed green leaves, sending out long bronze shoots that twine up and fill in gaps under pines or other trees which have lost their lower limbs. Slow growing. Plant at the same time on the sea side of a shelter belt of conifers.
E. pungens x ebbingei	A very handsome tall evergreen shrub of glossy green leaves with silver undersurfaces and sweetly scented small white tubular flowers in early autumn. On a warm sunny day they scent the garden.
Escallonia exoniensis	An immensely tall, tree-like shrub of pink buds opening up to white flowers in summer.

Escallonia 'Crimson Spire'

Makes a narrow hedge of dark green glossy foliage and crimson flowers. One of the best hedgers for the small garden by the sea.

Escallonia macrantha

The best escallonia for very exposed or cliff-top gardens with dark green gummy foliage and red flowers. Takes up a lot of room in the small garden because of its spreading root system.

Euonymus japonicus
5 to 15ft

The Spindleberry makes a splendid evergreen wind shelter even on pure sand. It is not hardy everywhere but where it grows well it is very tolerant of salt. Its great virtue is that quite large bushes can be moved successfully.

Griselinia littoralis
8 to 25ft

A very wind- and salt-tolerant evergreen of light-green rounded leaves. Not entirely frost-hardy, but forms the shelter of many gardens in Northern Ireland exposed to Irish Sea gales and on the Isle of Gigha off the West coast of Scotland. It is excellent for growing beneath trees and in dampish places. May be moved when 8ft tall.

Hebe brachysiphon
4 to 5ft

A stiff, erect evergreen with small, box-like leaves and short white flowers in June.

Hebe dieffenbachii
3 to 5ft

One of the best shrubs for extreme coastal exposure, quickly forming a large, hummocky bush with sea-green leaves and spikes of white flowers.

Hebe franciscana 'Blue Gem'
3 to 4ft

No other shrub is better able to withstand extreme cliff-top exposure and salt spray than this compact, waxy-leaved maritime shrub.

Hebe 'Lavender Queen'
4 to 6ft

This tall and vigorous hybrid with light green leaves and short spikes of pale lavender flowers fading to white, is a good shrub for sheltering other less hardy plants but should not be used in the first line of defence.

Hippophae rhamnoides
6 to 8ft

The Sea Buckthorn will grow in pure sand and is one of the best deciduous shrubs for extreme exposure even on the cold east coast. It has narrow silvery leaves, and orange berries if male and female plants are grown. Birds leave the berries alone.

Lonicera ledebouri
6 to 8ft

This erect, deciduous shrub with small red and yellow flowers grows very fast indeed at the sea's edge. Very common in wet places.

Lycium chinense
5 to 7ft

The Box Thorn is a valuable nurse plant in the teeth of gales and could be planted on the outside of a shelter belt to give protection to it. It is a scrambling climber with small purplish flowers followed by orange-scarlet fruits. Common on south and east coast cliffs.

Medicago arborea
5ft

The Moon Trefoil is an undistinguished shrub for exposed situations, with light-green leaves and deep-yellow pea flowers for much of the year. Very wind-tolerant but not entirely frost-hardy.

Olearia albida
6 to 8ft

This tall New Zealand shrub has tough, leathery leaves and off-white daisy flowers in August. It stands up well to salt-laden winds and is reasonably hardy.

Olearia haastii
4 to 5ft

The hardiest of the olearias and good on very cold coasts. Small oval grey leaves and off-white daisies in July.

Olearia macrodonta
4 to 6ft

Often called the New Zealand holly because of its toothed grey-green leaves. Corymbs of white daisy flowers in June. *O. mac. major* has larger leaves. Can have its annual growth reduced after flowering to keep it bushy.

Olearia solandri
5 to 6ft

A beautiful foliage shrub for producing a golden heath-like effect. Not entirely frost-hardy but makes a good hedge on milder coasts.

Phormium tenax
6 to 8ft

The New Zealand Flax has broad, sword-like leaves and tall arching flower spikes of coppery-red or yellow. It belongs to a tough race of maritime plants which make splendid wind-shelter in gardens on the west coast of Scotland.

Prunus spinosa
4 to 6ft

The well-known blackthorn with white flowers in spring on bare twiggy branches. Not recommended for gardens as it is liable to cause poisonous scratches on the gardener.

Rhododendron ponticum
10 to 20ft

Often called the common rhododendron owing to its abundant seeding on acid, peaty soil. Flowers pink or mauve. Makes good shelter on west coast.

Ribes alpinum
6 to 8ft

Makes dense, twiggy growth, offering nearly as much protection

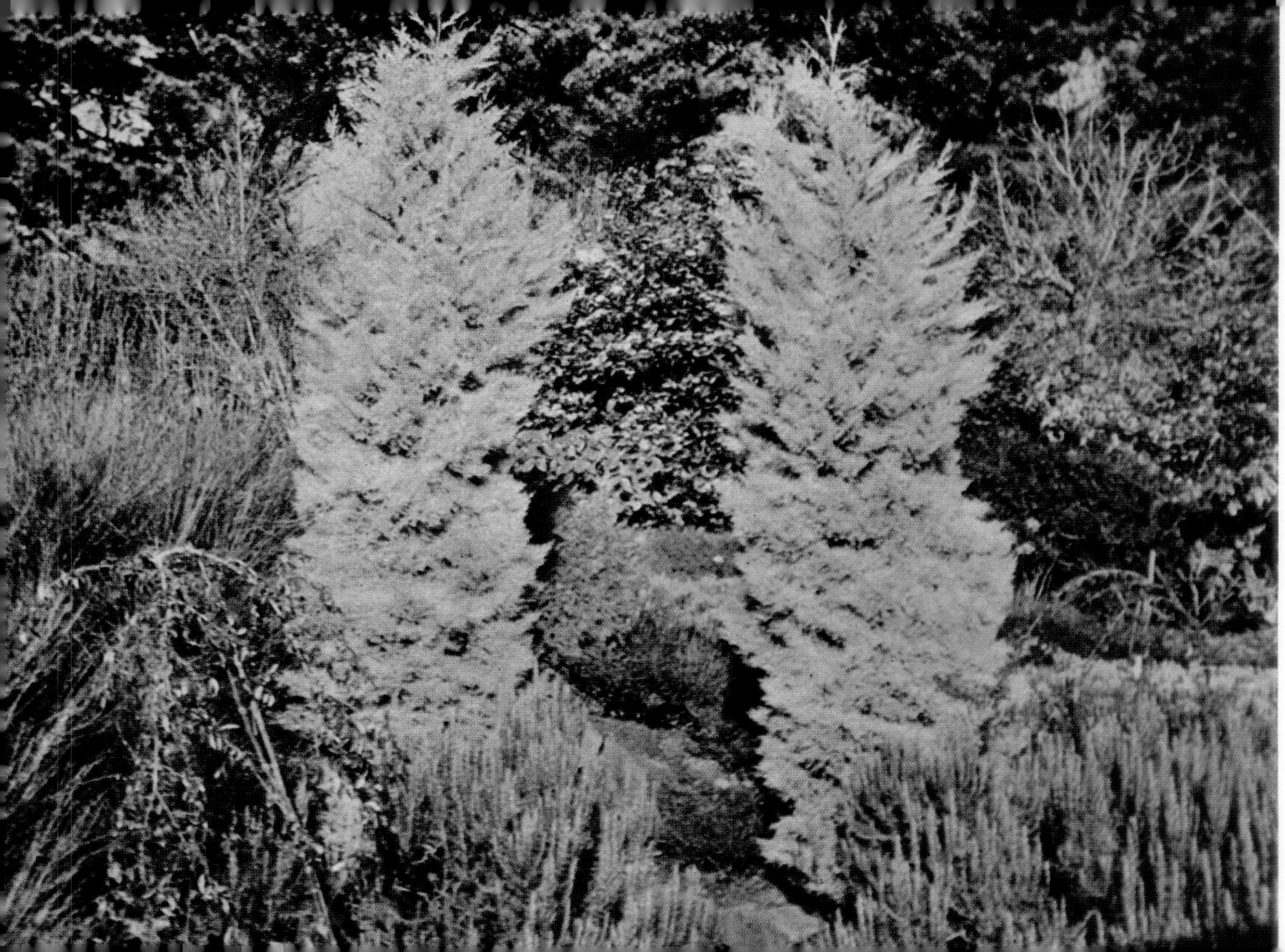

Page 35 : *Cupressus macrocarpa* 'Goldcrest'

Page 36: Genista canariensis in the author's garden

from wind in winter as it does when full of leaf in summer. The lower branches layer themselves to keep a hedge well filled at the bottom. One of the best hedging plants for northern coastal gardens.

Sambucus nigra
15 to 20ft

The common elder grows in extreme exposure, draping other trees and bushes to make an impenetrable screen. Its yellowish-white flowers are followed by abundant black fruits.

Senecio laxifolius
3 to 4ft

One of the toughest of seaside shrubs, with silver-grey leaves and yellow daisies in summer.

Senecio monroi
3ft

A valuable shrub for seaside planting, with small crinkled leaves, silvery-white underneath. Flowers are similar to those of *S. laxifolius* but flower three weeks later.

Senecio rotundifolius
6 to 8ft

A tall, large-leaved shrub of unusually fine architectural character, which succeeds in extreme exposure, but dislikes very dry soils and is not hardy enough for the colder coasts.

Tamarix gallica
8 to 10ft

Tamarisk is highly resistant to salt spray and prized for beach planting all over the world. It has graceful feathery foliage and pink plumes in August. Prune hard in spring to encourage bushy growth.

Ulex europaeus
4 to 6ft

Common gorse is one of the most valuable shelter shrubs for cliff-top planting. The freedom with which it seeds can be a welcome

c

attribute in a wild garden or a menace in a cultivated one.

Ulex europaeus plenus
3 to 4ft

The double gorse is a most effective spring-flowering shelter shrub, completely covered with golden-yellow flowers over a long period. It stands any amount of wind and salt.

3

INSTANT GARDENING

TODAY it is 'instant' everything. We are all wildly impatient and gardeners, most of them, are no exception. The owners of new plots of ground understandably cannot wait to see the bare earth covered and the middle-aged in retirement naturally want to see the results of their labours. Few people now plant for posterity. The incentive which inspired our ancestors to plant for their descendants is no longer so strong, for only the few now think of living permanently in a house they have bought or built. So it is that insecurity and uncertainty have crept even into our gardening lives.

In the last few years there has been a general rush to the coast to build either a holiday house or a home for retirement. Often the one develops into the other. One has only to motor around the coastline of Britain to be made aware of the large housing estates that are springing up like mushrooms in coastal districts. Soon land on the coast for building will be very scarce indeed, for there is something in the British nature that draws us to the sea.

In many cases it is an entirely fresh adventure, and newcomers to the coast have little idea of the problems awaiting them when they begin to garden near the sea. They may have spent most of their gardening lives in sheltered places inland, or in industrial towns where the problems are very different. By the sea, they will not have to face the severe and prolonged frost that may have plagued them inland, but there are other sorts of evils to combat, the greatest of which is the destructive salt-laden wind.

On new ground almost the first necessity may be to clear the ground, which is often a positive wilderness of brambles and nettles. Though many owners are still trying to clear the ground with a hook, this is a chore far better done with the aid of modern chemicals. Moreover, slashing about with a hook is about the worst treatment for those incurable optimists, the brambles, which will certainly come up stronger than ever in the ensuing years. Nettles, too, are not easily deterred. But try mixing up a solution of a brushwood killer such as SBK in a watering can, carefully following the maker's instructions (an overdose is no more effective than the specified amount) and spray it over the brambles and nettles. The result is very satisfactory, and though each may need a second dose this should see the last of them. And what a saving of precious time and labour!

Next in order of importance for 'quick results' I place the erection of artificial screening against the worst of the prevailing winds that strike the garden. The best types of shelter available today have been examined in the previous chapter and I consider that money cannot be better spent at the beginning than in investing in this kind of protection for young plants. If you are not good at this sort of job, it is better to employ skilled labour to erect the fencing, as the uprights that support the fence must be very firmly fixed into the ground before any fencing is attached. Gales can play havoc with a fence that is not strongly supported. It should not be necessary to surround the entire garden, like a barricade, but a few screens placed in strategic positions to filter the worst winds will work wonders in helping to get young plants established.

For 'quick results', shrubs and trees should be planted small. It is a dangerous fallacy to suppose that time will be saved by putting in large plants, or that a good windbreak will be established more quickly. Quite the contrary is the case. Small plants will have caught up their elders in a couple of years and will then grow twice as fast and be twice as strong.

GARDEN CENTRES

I suppose nothing has given more pleasure of recent years to thousands of gardeners than the arrival of garden centres where all manner of plants which have been grown in containers may be bought on the spot and carried away. The cost of carriage and packing would often be more than the price of the plants, so that garden centres which sell good plants ready to take away make possible a considerable saving.

The largest garden centre in Britain is at Syon House, Brentwood, Middlesex, but good ones are popping up all over the country. At these centres the customer can select his plant, take it home with him and plant it out, even if it is in full bloom, though plants in bud are a far better buy. To be able to carry the plant home in the car is a thrill for any keen gardener but particularly for the owner of a newly-acquired plot with much bare earth to cover, or for the possessor of a holiday house with only a week or two of planting time at his disposal. In a good garden centre the plants will be well grown and thoroughly hardened off. The plants should have had time to develop a root ball that will hold together when they are moved from the container into the garden soil, and remember that a plant that looks poor will certainly look a good deal worse when you come to plant it out. Not all container plants are container grown, often they have simply been grown in the

open nursery and put into containers to make them more sale-
able and attractive to the customer. I like the soil in the container to look well established, perhaps with a film of green
moss on the surface.

The disadvantages of these garden centres is, I feel, that the
range of plants is bound to suffer in time since only popular
plants of special appeal to the gardening public are likely to
be offered. Going round these centres, I have been disappointed not to find more quality plants for sale and it will
be a sad day if these were gradually to disappear. It is a pity,
too, that plants are not more clearly marked to show the type
of soil they grow best in, the lime-tolerant ones being kept distinct from the acid-soil lovers. It might not be in the interests
of the nurseryman to do so but it would certainly be to the
advantage of the customer. Very many amateur gardeners
who visit garden centres are often unaware that these enticing
plants will not grow for them.

Here, a word of warning to the novice at this kind of 'instant
gardening' may not come amiss. Most containers are expendable and are not intended to be planted into the ground with
the plant. If you buy a plant in a metal container it is cus-
tomary for the nurseryman to cut the container down one side
before you take it away, to make for easier removal when
planting. Should the container be of bitumised-paper or poly-
thene, place the plant and container into the hole already
prepared for it and slit the container on two sides from top
to bottom, then withdraw it carefully from under the plant.
It is always best to have the hole ready beforehand, making
it larger than the container, then add a little fertiliser with
some moistened peat, and water the hole well before easing
the plant out with as little disturbance of its roots as possible.
Then water again, fill in around the plant and firm the soil
with the foot and rake some loose soil around the plant. Should
the weather be dry, plants will need watering until new growth

is seen to start, and a spray over the leaves after a hot day or a drying wind will help the plant on its way. On very light soil a mulch of garden compost or moist peat around the plant will be a further insurance against loss.

Of all forms of 'instant gardening', the one most needed by gardeners on new properties, particularly those by the sea, is probably some sort of quick-growing hedge or screen. I read recently that modern gardens were becoming so small that hedges were out, but I very much doubt if the British gardener will so easily relinquish his one means of achieving a little privacy for himself and his property. Unlike the Americans, we value our privacy and the saying 'an Englishman's home is his castle' would have less point if his 'castle' were open to the public gaze. As soon as a new house is being built, almost the first question I am asked is 'What shall I use as a hedge'? If the garden is minute, perhaps the answer should be 'Some sort of artificial fence' which is immediately effective and takes up the least possible space. Where there is room, however, the owner is more likely to be looking for a living screen or hedge which will prove an asset to the garden but which will not take years to reach the required height.

I can think of no faster-growing hedge plant than *Cupressocyparis leylandii*, but it must be emphasised that this suffers badly from browning in extreme maritime exposure and should only be used where there is some shelter from the worst salt winds. Leyland's Cypress is the fastest growing conifer in the British Isles, indeed the fastest growing evergreen except for one or two eucalypts. It makes a splendid tall tree in next to no time and is ideal for concealing an ugly eyesore like those concrete horrors that are rising up everywhere to spoil our landscape. In my own case I am using it to screen off an ugly electric pole. As a hedger, there is nothing to beat it, it is the fastest grower of all. From its parents, *Cupressus macrocarpa* and *Chamaecyparis nootkatensis*, it inherits the best qualities of each, the speed of growth of *macrocarpa* with the hardiness of *nootkatensis*. One can expect growth to be at the rate of about 4ft a year. It remains bright green, suffering no die-back like *macrocarpa*, and remains dense right to the ground, a definite advantage this in very windy gardens. It stands trimming well, even with mechanical hedge-trimmers. The time to clip is the end of May or early June, but not after the longest day. Simply trim the sides until it has reached the required height. Plant 2½ft apart in March or April on any soil, light sand or heavy clay, but not in extreme cliff exposure.

The days of privet to form a boundary hedge for the seaside garden are fast disappearing. There are many more exciting hedgers and almost its only recommendation in my eyes is its cheapness. It is a soil-robber and this is particularly undesirable in small gardens where every inch of ground is valuable. It also needs trimming at least twice a year. But for the young, already heavily committed financially, I can see its attraction. A tamarisk hedge, however, is also cheap, since cuttings put straight into the ground in very early spring usually root and it will grow on excessively sandy soils with its feet washed by salt water. But it is deciduous, and does not make such a good hedge as one of the flowering escallonias. The erect E. Crimson Spire, with very dark foliage and bright crimson flowers, makes a solid 6ft hedge in four years. It is very wind- and salt-tolerant and does not take up much room, as its habit is tall and narrow. I recommend it for the small garden.

An attractive alternative is a hedge of the new hybrid brooms. In Scotland, where winds are very strong, they make more use of these hedges than we do in England. There I have seen the broom stand firm and unscathed in the fiercest gale and it has much to recommend it. It is indifferent to the soil it grows on, is easily and quickly raised from seed by the ordinary gardener and when in flower is truly spectacular, in a wide range of colours, red, pink, gold, white or cream and

Page 45 : Lath screens in the author's garden

Page 46: (*above*) *Santolina virens* alternates with *Helichrysum plicatum*; (*below*) Daffodils and heather in the author's garden

Page 47 (*above*) *Cupressocyparis leylandii* clothed to the ground; (*below*) *Cupressus macrocarpa* Lutea, the most salt-tolerant conifer for coastal planting

Page 48: (above) The wind and salt tolerant *Olearia traversii*; (below) Sea Buckthorn at the water's edge

many bi-colours. The seed should be soaked overnight, which is less trouble than scratching the surface of each and every seed and just as effective. Sow the seed ½in deep in drills in the open ground in September.

By the following April, the small plants may be moved to their permanent quarters, 18in apart in the hedge line. Always transplant the small seedlings with care, as few plants resent root disturbance more than the broom. If the drill is watered beforehand then there is a chance of lifting the plants intact with a ball of soil. After the broom's first flowering, the top should be cut level with the shears and the sides trimmed to remove as many seed pods as possible. The second year the height should be reduced to about 18in and a few inches taken off the sides. This should get rid of most of the seed pods so that the plant's energies are not wasted in setting seed. In subsequent years remove a great many of the seed pods but do not cut into old, hard wood. Such a hedge gives years of pleasure and protection in very windy districts by the sea.

I never cease to extol the elaeagnus for seaside planting. One that is excellent for wind resistance near the sea is *Elaegnus x ebbingei*, a tall, very fast-growing shrub with dark green, glossy leaves with silver reverse. We use it largely in our garden for giving shelter against the gales and it is first-class for hedging. Plant 2½ft apart in single rows.

I deal at some length in a later chapter (Chapter 9) with the rapid-growing eucalyptus because I feel they make such unusual and welcome additions to any garden in which they are grown. They are perfectly successful in seaside gardens provided they are kept out of the wind. I should also stress what a gift these beautiful evergreen trees are for the impatient gardener, for a growth of 4 to 5ft a year is not uncommon. They are not difficult to grow and very exciting to watch in their rapid growth.

Another very fast-growing plant for seaside planting is the

Tree Lupin, *Lupinus arboreus*. Unlike the herbaceous lupin, it grows well on both limy and acid soils and revels in the warmth of sand. I have seen huge specimens full of flower on almost pure sand at the sea's edge. Tree Lupins are quickly rewarding, growing very fast indeed with deliciously scented spikes of flower from May to July. Never give them VIP treatment; they last longer and flower more profusely on poor ground. Though they are not long-lived, they are prodigious seeders, so that it is worth starting with a really good kind. I like best a bright sunshine yellow such as 'Golden Spire'. Seed may be sown direct into the ground, or into peat pots which can be planted into the garden, pot and plant, for, like the broom, the lupin resents any disturbance of its roots.

For quick effect among slow-growing shrubs, or in a mixed border of perennial plants, the impatient gardener should consider the Tree Mallow, *Lavatera olbia rosea*, with large satiny-pink flowers rather like those of the hollyhock. I have always marvelled at the amazing wind- and salt-tolerance of all the mallow tribe, and I have seen the Tree Mallow thoroughly happy high up on a windy site above the sea. It will grow in any soil but it is not always long-lived. After five or six years it is best replaced. A sturdy 6in plant will be all of 5ft by the end of its first season and it has a long flowering season from early July until October. In our own garden, bushes have reached 6ft with a spread of 3 to 4ft and have needed the support of stakes against the recurring gales. Self-sown seedlings are found about the garden but any special one must be propagated from cuttings. 'Rosea' has pale green leaves and rose-coloured flowers, but there is also a particularly fine form with wine-red stems and flowers of a deep purplish-pink.

The hebes, or shrubby veronicas to many of us, are a great help in furnishing the new seaside garden. A few bits and pieces taken from a friend's garden will quickly root, even in a glass of water, making small bushes in their second year. *H. franciscana* Blue Gem and *H. dieffenbachii* are two of the very best for extreme exposure, standing wind and salt with impunity, while the lovely 'Miss Fittall', with long, tapering, lavender spikes, is one of the hardiest of the large-flowered garden hybrids. Many of those with the brightest colours are regrettably frost-tender and must have shelter from cold winds, but they are such beautiful late-flowering shrubs, up to Christmas in a mild climate, that they are worth the trouble of taking cuttings in a frame and planting them in the garden when all danger of frost is past.

When I am asked to suggest a rapid climber to cover a wall the same year, I think immediately of that beautiful but unusual climber, *Cobaea scandens*. Its rate of growth is phenomenal. It is usually treated as a half-hardy annual but in many seaside gardens I have known it frequently over-winters, flowering early and fruiting heavily. The broadly shaped, bell-like flowers are like those of a Canterbury Bell. They open jade green, become tinged with lavender and the colour deepens until the whole corolla is rich violet. But this is not all. When these fall, the large calyx cups remain, looking like green flowers, and should the summer be a hot one, then plum-shaped fruits appear, gradually turning to gold. I think it is one of Nature's fantasies, a most fascinating plant. And it is easy to grow. You can sow seed in individual peat pots in February in a greenhouse where the temperature does not drop below 45 degrees, and by May the plants may be put out, pots and all, into their permanent position against a wall. The first few weeks of its outdoor life are, I find, the most tricky but a cane will help it to climb and then it grows rapidly to cover the wall the same summer. I grew the Cobaea up a 'Mermaid' rose but it threatened to swamp the rose and had to be restrained, for once it starts there is no stopping it.

Annuals, of course, are one of the quickest ways of getting

colour into a new garden. Though our own garden is given over largely to flowering shrubs and hardy perennial plants, I remember how successful was an original planting of the annual *Lavatera trimestris*. There is not a mallow that does not like and thrive on sea air and this annual bushy plant, often 3 to 4ft tall, with large, pink, trumpet-like flowers which open fully and last all summer, proved very successful indeed, filtering the wind and seemingly impervious to the salt that drifted over the garden. Sow it about the garden from March to May where you want it to flower. It will give you a feast of colour while the new garden is getting under way. Many other annuals may grow in your seaside garden but no one better than this.

4

STAR PLANTS
BY THE SEA

SOME plants, like humans, have star quality. They seem
groomed for stardom. Their flower or their leaves have
that poise and 'extra something' we demand from the
most glamorous of our film stars. Such plants should always
look their best, as though conscious that always 'the show must
go on'. They are often the show pieces in our gardens, for
every gardener is a showman at heart and not without vanity.
There are many plants which make first-rate show pieces,
some are easy-going while others ask for just that special bit
of skill and care that adds to the zest of growing them.

I would describe a show piece as one that one returns to
again and again with infinite pleasure, and since many of
those I have in mind are not often seen in inland gardens they
come in for more than ordinary appreciation in seaside gardens.
They give their owners a special pleasure but they also provide a useful talking-point for visitors. Even the dullest visitor
comes alive when confronted with one such plant. Then ques-
tions come thick and fast. How hardy is it? Could I grow it
in my garden? What sort of soil does it need? It reminds one

of the very successful flower-arrangement on the dinner-table that sets the tongues wagging.

Just as a Pineapple Plant from Chile, with the strange name of *Puya berteronia*, with bright green and peacock-blue flowers, flowering for the sixth time in its forty odd years, was the star plant of a recent Chelsea Show—judging by the crowds who gazed in fascination at this unusual plant—so there are star plants of lesser magnitude to grace gardens by the sea.

Visitors to the milder parts of Britain, and to the west coasts of Scotland and Ireland, are often astonished to come across an exotic-looking plant with blue-green, yucca-like leaves, though not spinetipped as in a yucca, and enormous flower-stems growing at the most impossible angles. This is the Mexican *Beschorneria yuccoides*, whose great leaning stems, often 6 to 8ft long, are bright shrimp-pink throughout and contrast vividly with the drooping flowers which, though comparatively small for so large a plant, are green tinged with yellow and draped with rose-red bracts. The handsome leaves add to its attraction. Whether you admire it or not, it is a plant not easily forgotten in a coastal garden during May and June.

I thought it something of a compliment to the New Zealand Flax, *Phormium tenax*, when I saw it included recently in an article on plants of aristocratic mien, but there is no doubt that its variegated form entitles it to a place among the stars. This very handsome variety of *P. tenax*, with sword-like, rigid leaves, 6 or 7ft long, striped lengthwise with green and yellow, is an eye-catcher, with great towering flower-stalks carrying coppery-red flowers. It is most striking in an isolated position with the sea behind it, for salt and wind have little effect upon it. It may not be happy everywhere but it is certainly hardy in the west, as massive clumps seen as far north as Arran prove. It is an old plant in gardens, one of the many introductions of Sir Joseph Banks from the southern hemisphere.

Plant the Pokeweed in your garden and whether the reaction of visitors is one of curiosity, admiration or dislike, it will certainly not be ignored. To my surprise, this American plant, *Phytolacca americana* (*P. decandra*), suddenly appeared in my garden. It shot up to 4 or 5ft and the flowers, small and a slightly grubby white, were suffused first with green and later on with pink. At this stage I merely wondered what it could be, so surprising was the apparition among other border plants. In autumn, it immediately became more interesting as the insignificant flowers all down the tall stalk were transformed into purplish-black, glistening fruits and the whole thing resembled a spike laden with gleaming blackberries, At the same time I noticed that the soft green leaves were turning a shade of violet, and with the coming of winter the whole thing disappeared underground. The sap from the thong-like roots was used by the Indians in North America as an emetic and its highly-coloured juice has given it the name of the Ink Plant. Many, I know, will disagree with me for putting it among my star plants, but anyone interested in distinctive plants might well include it, not in a border of more beautiful herbaceous plants but to form a clump among shrubs or in the wilder part of a garden. It should not be grown where children play as many parts of the plants are said to be poisonous.

Whatever may be said of the Pokeweed, I doubt if anyone will dispute my inclusion of one of the yuccas among star plants for a seaside garden. These are seaside plants *par excellence* and will thrive even on sand dunes in full exposure to salt-laden gales. For the patient gardener who does not mind waiting for the spectacular display of the stately *Y. gloriosa*, there is no lovelier yucca, but unfortunately the flowering periods of this stem-forming plant are several years apart and what is even more exasperating, as has happened in my own garden, the plant sometimes tries to flower in mid-winter when the opening buds are destroyed by bad weather. But the star

plant, which delights many a seaside gardener with an almost
annual show in August of 6ft spikes of creamy-white bells
standing away from the main stem in short sprays, is *Y. filamentosa*. Some of the finest of these plants that I know of
grow in gardens on the coast of Galloway. Though salt-laden
gales sweep over them, they seem able to withstand any storm
without support and last year's stalks were still standing among
the new flower-stems. The worse that happens is a shredding
of the tips of the long pointed leaves. *Y. filamentosa*, unlike
Y. gloriosa, forms no central stem. The rosettes of blue-green
leaves and flower-stems all rise from ground level and annual
increase is from a sideways spreading of the crowns. Flowers
are produced early in the plant's life and recur annually with
rare exceptions, a great gain over the occasional flowering of
Y. gloriosa.

A yucca makes an ornamental addition to a garden and is
worth siting in a key position where it can be left to form
large clumps. I think April gives the best chance of success.
Plant the rosettes of *Y. filamentosa* so that the crown is just
sitting on the surface, but tread the roots firmly and if a dry
spell should follow planting, give it a soaking or two to get
it started. Yuccas like plenty of light and air and good drainage.
Wet and boggy soils are abhorrent to them. I have a bed of
yuccas on a lawn and, because weeding is made dangerous
by the sharp-pointed leaves, I grow *Lamium galeobdolon
variegatum* and *Campanula porscharskyana* as ground cover.
No weeds are able to penetrate these irrepressible plants. Perhaps the very vigorous lamium was a mistake, since it is now
attempting to festoon the yuccas with its trailing arms, but in
winter, when we have only the yucca leaves for company, its
silvered leaves glisten with a brilliance that brings the bed
alive.

Beneath a picture of the beautiful *Convolvulus cneorum* I
read the caption 'A half-hardy sub-shrub from Southern

Page 57: (above) Cordy-
ine australis (Dracaena
Palm) in flower; (below)
a stand of Elaeagnus
macrophylla

Page 58: (above) Silver-leaved *Santolina incana*; (below) *Eryngium pro-teiflorum* in its Mexican home

Europe that needs a cold greenhouse' and I thought how fortunate are we seaside gardeners who can safely grow it in the
open. For though it is a little tender and unsuited for cold inland gardens, it stands full exposure on the coast in mild localities. It may be that the silky hairs that clothe each leaf surface
enable it to withstand both wind and salt. Its beautiful satiny
leaves are agleam with a metallic silver and clusters of pink
buds unfurl to pure white, open flowers like a convolvulus,
but this small compact shrub is no dangerous spreader like
the pernicious bindweed and a star plant for a garden by the
sea. It is easily propagated from cuttings and it is as well to
keep a few plants in reserve in case of accidents, for it is too
good a plant to be missing from any garden where it can be
grown.

One's really worthwhile discoveries are made, only too often,
some years too late. This is the case with shrubs that take a
long time to reach maturity. The beautiful *Elaeagnus pungens
maculata* is one such shrub. It cannot be planted too soon,
for even in infancy it seems groomed for stardom. I cannot
think of a more striking winter shrub for a seaside garden.
Like all these New Zealand shrubs, it seems specially adapted
to withstand wind and salt, and few other shrubs better resist
drought or do so well on dry, sandy soil. It is a real scene-
stealer and should be planted in a strategic position with an
eye to the future when it will reach a height of 8 to 10ft with
a wide spread, though it will take years to do this. It is, I feel,
quite the showiest of all variegated shrubs, its highly polished
leaves with green margins being heavily splashed with yellow
and gold, and when a wintry sun strikes it there is no doubt
whatever that here is a plant of star quality.

But winter has scarcely left us when my star plant for early
spring comes into its own and lasts for months. This is the
evergreen shrubby spurge, *Euphorbia wulfenii*. In our seaside garden, February is not too soon to visit it. All through

D

the year it has carried its long arms densely clothed at the tips with handsome, blue-green foliage, but in very early spring there is the excitement of watching to see which of those great arms is going to flower. When the tips arch tightly over, so firmly that to straighten them would be to break them, then there is definite expectation of those huge, erect, love-bird green trusses, for these trusses with an orange eye, sometimes as much as a foot long, straighten of their own accord in a truly amazing manner. So exotic are they, and so striking their effect in a garden scarcely emerging from its winter sleep, that it is impossible to over-rate their value.

It is a plant so full of character that it should have a position where it is not muddled up with other plants. An excellent situation is on a wide, paved area or at some strategic corner. It puts up with poor soil, but in favoured localities, as near the sea, it will make massive growth, some 5ft through. If it should be thought to take up too much room in the limited space of a small garden, then the dwarf, more compact *E. characias* would be better. It is quite as beautiful, with a chocolate-brown eye and its foliage is particularly blue. I cut off the long arms of these spurges as soon as they have gone out of flower. Fresh growth appears from the middle of the plant, and though our plants have been with us now for over ten years I do wonder sometimes how much longer they can stand this hard pruning. Fortunately, they often produce self-sown seedlings. *E. epithymoides*, a wee spurge with yellow bracts of dazzling brightness in the spring sunshine, brings its own star quality into the small garden.

Many of our choice plants have come to us from South Africa and when *Crocosmia masonorum* came to this country a few years ago many thought its hardiness was suspect. But I have known it over-winter in the open in many seaside gardens up and down the country, particularly where the soil has been light and well-drained, so that it has not been necessary to lift and store the corms as was originally suggested. Its immense flowers resemble those of a giant montbretia, but its brilliant colouring and noble bearing are so striking that here the resemblance ends. At around 2ft, the stiff stems bend over, arching out to perhaps another 9in, and are set with magnificent, flame-orange flowers during July and August. This will make a splendid eye-catching show if a dozen or more corms are planted in a group. In its native land it is called the Golden Swan Tritonia, perhaps from the graceful curve of its neck.

Another most beautiful plant from South Africa, the Watsonia, is only rarely seen in this country because here it is on the borderline of hardiness. In places with a mild climate, as in south-west England, on the west coast of Scotland and in parts of Ireland, Watsonia can be grown as outdoor perennials and I remember my astonishment one August to find them flowering with abandon in a garden not far from Cape Wrath in Scotland, where the owners told me they had come safely through 15 degrees of frost without protection and were seeding about the garden. They were growing in a sandy loam, enriched with peat and leaf mould, in a sunny, well-drained situation, though they like abundant water when coming into flower. These were *Watsonia Beatricis* with many vivid, flame-coloured, funnel-shaped flowers opening at the same time on a 3ft stem and with leaves like a gladiolus. In their native South Africa they grow in many shades of mauve, orange and flame, as well as white. Only the favoured few can grow them and for them it is an opportunity not to be missed.

The difficulty of propagating *Romneya coulteri*, the Californian Tree Poppy, is often claimed by the amateur gardener to be the reason why it is omitted from the garden. It also occupies a good deal of room once it has become established and I have known it grow beneath a stone-flagged path in its desire to get to the other side. All this may account for the infrequency with which one comes across this most handsome, late-summer flowering, sub-shrubby, perennial plant, which is hardy in all but the coldest localities and is lime-tolerant. It will not be suitable for positions exposed to direct salt wind off the sea; those white poppy flowers, often as much as 5in across and looking for all the world like crimped tissue paper, would be torn to shreds by the first gale in full exposure, but many a seaside garden has sufficient shelter and the room to grow this outstanding plant. With its huge scented flowers, rigid stems and deeply-divided glaucous leaves it is a plant of star quality, both in the garden and in the house, where its beautiful flowers last for many days in water. Many years ago I was lunching at a well-known public school when my neighbour, pointing to a large vase of these lovely flowers, said how much he admired the single paeonies which he took them to be, and this was understandable since *romyeya* has a boss of golden stamens similar to that which is so pronounced a feature of the single white paeony.

Propagation can be from root cuttings, and I have rarely failed with these. Cut off pieces of root, 2 to 3in long, and insert them in very gritty builder's sand in pots in late summer. They can then be grown on in a cold greenhouse until the spring, when they may be planted out into the garden after all chance of frost is past. In this way they suffer no disturbance of the roots. An old gardener's tip is simply to spade off one of the upright glaucous stems on either side, leaving the plant *in situ* until the spring, when it will have made a new plant ready for removal to its permanent quarters. Once the plant is established it should be cut back to ground level each year in the spring.

Among my own favourite 'stars', and one I recommend for east coast gardens in particular, is Kniphofia 'Torchlight'. All red-hot pokers love sea air, do not object to the stiffest winds and tolerate salt drifting in off the sea. If different varieties

are chosen they will flower from May until October. It is a
fallacy to suppose that the east coast of England is so bleak,
so windswept and so dry that herbaceous plants will not flourish
there when such plants do well on the north-east coast at Whit-
ley Bay. The particular value of Kniphofia 'Torchlight' lies
not only in its late October flowering but in the spectacular,
triangular-shaped, orange-red pokers on a broad yellow base,
which make a splendid show in the late summer garden by the
sea. It is a particularly robust, strong-growing variety; an
established clump will carry thirty or more tall spikes of flower.
The kniphofias prefer a warm sandy, well-drained soil but
come to no harm in climates of heavier rainfall if their leaves
are bunched together into a sort of wigwam in early winter,
to prevent the rain or snow penetrating the centre of the plant.
In spring, the leaves can be untied to fall back into their
natural position.

Gardeners in warm seaside gardens should not miss the
opportunity of growing the brilliant Tigridias, planting them
in a sunny sheltered spot in spring. *T. pavonia*, called the Tiger
flower because of its spotted blooms, is a native of mountain
regions of Mexico and Peru. It grows 1 to 2ft tall, with orange-
scarlet flowers often with crimson spots, from July to September. There are various forms in shades of yellow, orange,
reddish crimson and white, some spotted and some without
spots. All are brilliantly coloured, but they last only one day,
though six or more flowers are produced from the one corm.
People tell me how sad it is that their gorgeous flowers last
for so short a time, and it is sad if you are away at work all
day only to be told on your return in the evening how mar-
vellous they were at mid-day. Since the amount of sunshine
influences their flowering, they do well in a hot summer, but
a place against a sunny wall sheltered from cold winds is
enough to induce a succession of exceedingly beautiful and
brightly coloured flowers. Although gardening books often

stress the necessity of a warm sunny spot, we are not told often enough that, like the gladiolus, the tigridia appreciates some watering around the plants as soon as it shows signs of budding. And like the gladiolus, corms should be lifted and stored each winter if the climate is unkind and the soil a heavy one. Winter wet is their enemy.

I can think of no other flower of such delicately exotic beauty, or more groomed for stardom in early autumn and even into November, than the beautiful pink *Nerine bowdenii*, and many a seaside garden owes its beauty at this dullest time of the gardening year to great masses of the pink nerine. It is a constant source of amazement to me that this 'hot-house-looking' flower is at its best just when the garden is beginning its winter sleep. There is something ethereal and magical about the pink nerine, with its umbels of from six to eight flowers borne on sturdy 18in stems, and the pink petals beautifully curled with a darker central streak. The best is Fenwick's Variety with larger flowers of deeper rose-pink, but *N. bowdenii* is good enough for most of us.

Nerines, though not prodigal of leaves, are not born without them; they produce most of their foliage in the spring and once they start to flower it is a joy to gardeners to see how rapidly the bulbs increase. And, unlike *Amaryllis belladonna*, they continue to flower with great regularity each autumn. But do not be disappointed should they not flower their first season, roots must become crowded if the plants are to flower well. They do not need the shelter of a sunny wall except in the colder districts, but though our nerines have had no protection of any sort, it is wisest not to risk these precious bulbs on the coldest coasts without a covering of peat as soon as they have gone out of flower in December. They make a beautiful and colourful fringe to a narrow border at the base of a wall, but clumps of bulbs do very well indeed in a sheltered spot at the front of shrub borders and are particularly attractive when

associated with the grey foliage of plants like *Teucrium fruticans*, artemisias, *Senecio cineraria* or *Senecio leucostachys*.

If you must divide them, there is apparently only a very
short period in late February or early March when the nerine
is dormant and that is the time to lift and divide them.
Recently, however, in September, I was given the precious
gift of a bag of these bulbs that had remained in their bag
for some weeks previously, and within three weeks of planting
them in my garden they were a mass of flower. Whether they
will miss a season before flowering again we shall have to wait
and see. There is no other plant in our garden that gives me
lovelier cut flowers well into November and the blooms last a
good ten days in water.

Should you be interested in growing a unique and spectacular plant, groomed for stardom in the garden or for fresh or
dried arrangements, then you will certainly try the beautiful
but difficult *Eryngium proteiflorum*. Other spellings occur in
catalogues but this is the spelling given by Kew. Mr Elcock,
who spent over twenty years in Mexico, tells me that he discovered 'Rosa de la Montana', as it was known locally, on the
slopes of the volcanic Popocatepétl in Mexico, at a height of
some 12-14,000ft where the temperature drops well below
freezing. A colony of these eryngiums was growing in full
sun on small hillocks of volcanic shale amidst tufts of a tough-
looking grass. The striking flowers appear in July onwards,
with large bracts of a delicate sea-green surrounding the central cone of steely blue. The pale 2ft flower stalk rises from a
sculptured-looking cluster of long, narrow blue-green leaves
armed with vicious little spines down the sides. Each strong
stalk can carry a head of up to four flowers, of which the
central one is the largest and is often 4 to 5in across.

This plant is an absolute gift for flower arrangers, whether
cut fresh from the garden or dried, but it is definitely an outdoor plant. In its native habitat on volcanic shale, *Eryngium*

proteiflorum endures a daily downpour of torrential rain from May to October, followed by a completely dry six months. While these conditions are difficult to simulate in our gardens in this country the essentials are : (i) Full sun; (ii) light porous soil; (iii) frequent watering in summer; (iv) keeping its feet dry in winter. I think it suffers more from the dampness of our winters than from the cold. Sandy shore gardens would seem to supply most of this eryngium's needs, if watering can be carried out in summer.

Seed, originally sent home to this country by Mr Elcock, is procurable from Messrs Thompson & Morgan, and should be sown in spring in 'JiffyPots' to avoid transplating which may prove fatal. Sow in cool conditions such as are recommended for hardy perennials. Young seedlings are very susceptible to damping off. The young plants should have the protection of a cold frame or greenhouse during their first winter and be transplanted to a position in full sun the following spring. I believe we should all grow one or two plants in large pots for over-wintering in a cold greenhouse; the rest should take pot luck in the garden. This eryngium could well be the star plant of your seaside garden.

If I have left to the last the beautiful *Ceanothus arboreus* Trewithen Blue, it is to bring to the attention of seaside gardeners this most striking of blue-flowered, hardy shrubs. Remarkably wind-tolerant and fast-growing, it delights with a continuous succession of intense blue flower spikes over a long period from spring to autumn—a star shrub without a rival for seaside gardens.

5

PRUNING PAYS

AN old gardener's saying, as true today as when it was said many years ago, is that 'Growth follows the knife'. Very broadly speaking, we prune to maintain or prolong the vitality of the plant, to keep it within bounds, or to direct its energies into flowering. Of all gardening operations, pruning must be one of the least understood and so we find that those in doubt leave it alone, often with dire results.

The chief difficulty seems to lie in determining the *time* to prune. Gardeners tell me they are afraid to prune because they do not know *when* it should be done. So, they leave things alone, with the result that the strongest growers swamp the less robust, there is a lot of dead and diseased wood about, flowering is diminished, and a few neglected shrubs even fail to flower at all.

Very generally speaking, shrubs that flower in spring or before mid-summer do so on old wood, while those that bloom after mid-summer do so on new wood. So, in general, a simple rule is to prune the first, ie the early flowerers, immediately after they have flowered, and to leave the latter, ie those blooming after mid-summer, for pruning in winter dormancy, often very early in the spring.

Since we are here concerned with shrubs that do well in

seaside gardens, I shall confine my remarks to these. Wind-break shrubs, for instance, whose sole function it is to protect more worthwhile plants from wind and salt, scarcely need attention from us. The winds see to that. We have only to study those shorn and ill-shaped trees and bushes on some exposed coast to see how cruelly salt-laden gales have done the pruning for us. To seaward they have no leaves at all, the buds have literally been rubbed out by the force of onshore winds, and only on the sheltered side, away from the sea, do branches stretch out towards the land and are the leaves allowed to grow. This is Nature's way at its most brutal. Trees and shrubs grown for wind protection in extreme exposure rarely escape disfigurement on the sea side, but branches browned and scorched by salt, however unsightly, should not be removed, for these give shelter against future destructive gales.

Man's pruning, with secateurs or saw, is an altogether less ruthless affair than Nature's, although old and neglected bushes which have become an eyesore may be drastically pruned in the hope that they will break again from the base. If they do not, there is no alternative to having them out. But after an abnormal winter it is as well to wait awhile. In 1963, when escallonias in our garden were killed to the ground by prolonged bitter weather, they came again from the roots and today are as vigorous and full of flower as ever.

After a wet summer, such as we frequently have in this country, gardens can look very hirsute and blowsy, so that it is tempting to go round shortening long growths and generally tidying up, but each shrub must be treated on its merits and we should be careful not to remove branches that will bear next season's flowers in our quest for tidiness.

There can be no garden by the sea in which a buddleia will not flourish, though even buddleias vary in their pruning. The common one in gardens is *B. davidii*, or its hybrids. I like

to shorten its long, flowered branches by 18in in the autumn,
before winter gales take their toll and cause excessive rocking of
the roots. This also does away with the unattractive, gawky
appearance it presents, a mass of dead sticks in winter, but the
main pruning should always be done in very early spring,
February or early March. It pays to be really drastic with the
buddleias, cutting hard back to three or four buds from the
base. Old bushes will look bare for a week or two but they will
flower all the better with new flowering shoots, 5 or 6ft long,
by mid-summer. The graceful, cascading *B. alternifolia*, on
the other hand, does not care for such brutal treatment and
only needs a trim or shortening of its trailing branches and,
should this be necessary, it is best done immediately after
flowering in June. *B. globosa*, the Orange Ball Bush, was the
first buddleia ever to arrive in Britain. It dislikes hard pruning,
since the following year's flowers are borne on the current
year's growth, and if any pruning is deemed necessary it should
be completed just after it has gone out of flower.

Whatever one feels about the use of hydrangeas for public
functions, there can be no doubt whatever that they are superb
flowering shrubs for gardens by the sea, both the mopheads and
the lacecaps. No race of plants contributes more to late summer
colour over a long period, especially in moist climates, than
H. macrophylla. Hydrangeas are surprisingly tolerant of wind
and unique among large-leaved, deciduous shrubs for the way
in which they stand up to coastal exposure, but it is unfortunate that owners of average-sized or even small gardens too
often seem to plant large varieties which make immense
bushes that have to be drastically curtailed, rather than some
of the dwarf, compact kinds which are available. This is particularly unfortunate since hydrangeas dislike heavy pruning
at any time, for much valuable flowering wood is sacrificed
in the process. If a hydrangea bush gets too big for its position,
simply move it with a ball of soil, like a rhododendron, but do

not cut it hard back. If you do, it will never forgive you. The
best you can do with an old neglected bush that cannot be
moved is to shorten half the long shoots one year and the
other half the year following. In this way you will at least
get some flowers. Pruning should be carried out in spring and
consists of removing the dusty brown flowers that have served
to protect the buds beneath from winter's cold, removing any
growths thinner than a pencil which have little hope of ever
bearing a flower, cutting out all dead wood, but taking extreme care not to remove the plump buds towards the tops of
the stout stems, as it is from these that the flowers will be produced.

H. paniculata calls for quite different treatment. This very
distinct and hardy species has massive, cone-shaped bunches
of creamy-white sterile flowers that fade to pink. Should truly
enormous inflorescences, so popular today, be required, then
this hydrangea may be cut almost to ground level. If, however,
a bush is lightly pruned, the flowers will be smaller but there
will be many more of them. You can take your choice. Where
it is a large-flowered bush among herbaceous perennial plants
in a border, severe pruning is often practised, but in many
gardens on the west and north coasts of Scotland, where the
hardy *H. paniculata* has never been pruned, large tree-like
specimens carry numbers of attractive upright flowers into
late autumn.

No regular annual pruning is necessary with the shrubby
hebes, though leggy bushes may be cut back quite severely in
spring. These will flower later, and even continue in flower
until Christmas in a mild season.

Strong growing escallonias such as *E. macrantha*, *E. in-
gramii*, Crimson Spire, Red hedger and C. F. Ball, make good
protective hedges for seaside gardens. Their pruning should
be carried out immediately after the main flush of flower is
over, not later than August in exposed situations, to allow

them to make new growth before winter sets in. Hedges that are trimmed back late in autumn often suffer die-back, are greatly weakened when exposed to salt-laden gales, and their flowering the following season is much reduced. We lost a hedge of *E. rubra* that formed our western boundary in this way. Many beautiful hybrids, such as Apple Blossom, Donard Radiance, Donard Star and others, give superb results after a severe pruning of long shoots in spring. Most gardeners do not care to mete out this hard treatment, though a shrub growing beside a path may need to be curtailed and this can be done with impunity.

A few shrubs really enjoy harsh pruning. When our gardener, one spring, cut back a large straggling bush of the scented honeysuckle, *Lonicera halliana*, so that not a green leaf remained, I feared for its survival, but it did not deter this rampant climber from putting on a beautiful show of its biscuit-coloured flowers from June until the autumn.

The Tree Mallow, *Lavatera olbia*, is a splendid seaside shrub and much in demand for new gardens by the sea since it is so fast growing in its first season. It will grow 5ft in a season and I am often amazed at the way members of the mallow family put up with winds on the coast. *Lavatera olbia rosea* is a bright pink but there is, too, a delightful dark magenta one with red stems. The mallows come readily from seed but any particularly fine variety may be propagated from cuttings. Cut over a bush in autumn, shortening the long flowered shoots to prevent winter damage, and again in spring when it should be cut down to about 3ft from the ground to encourage an abundance of its mallow-pink flowers.

The cistus, or rock rose, requires no regular pruning, though I like to pinch back the tips of the shoots after flowering to promote a bushier habit. The same treatment may be applied to the pretty, yellow-flowered *Coronilla glauca*, though no particular time can be specified since this is a shrub that flowers at different times according to the coast on which it grows. In the south and west it will flower all winter, while on the colder east coast it starts to flower in late spring.

Tamarisks, which are among the most useful deciduous shrubs for excessively sandy places including sand dunes, stand a lot of pruning and if we could only bring ourselves to do this regularly we should have better furnished plants. Most tamarisks, and this includes the summer-flowering *Tamarix gallica* and *T. pentandra*, should be pruned hard in April, while *T. parviflora,* in my opinion the loveliest of them all and one I would like to see planted more often in seaside gardens, is pruned only after it has flowered in April and May with beautiful reddish-purple buds opening to deep pink plumes of flower.

While you can drastically cut back the tamarisks and they are all the better for it, such treatment would ruin *Viburnum tinus*, the laurustinus. This is not commonly regarded as a seaside shrub, yet it does very well indeed when grown by the sea, as at Bournemouth where it is extensively planted. I once watched a man clipping over a bush so that the result was a uniform, round bush of symmetrical shape, but I doubt very much if it produced those lovely flat heads of white lacy flowers on reddish stems that deck a free-grown bush of this most valuable winter-flowering evergreen. The laurustinus should never be severely pruned, only gently shaped if necessary with secateurs. In a sheltered garden in a mild locality it would be worth trying one of the more tender laurustinus, such as *V.t. lucidum*. It grows fast and has larger, more handsome flowers and nicely polished leaves.

Another valuable winter-flowerer is *Garrya elliptica*. In the south-west I have seen great stands in the open garden where it sheltered other more tender shrubs, though it is commonly planted against a wall where a male plant, which has longer, silver-grey catkins than the female, is draped with these very early in the year. Pruning should be carried out as soon as the catkins are past their best, never in the summer or the next season's catkins will be sacrificed. To prevent the heavy appearance this shrub frequently adopts over the years, long shoots can be cut right out and this makes a far more attractive plant.

Olearias, the daisy bushes from New Zealand, stand a good deal of regular annual pruning. Indeed the beautiful hybrid, *O. scilloniensis*, will produce a mass of dazzling white flowers in early spring if its flowering shoots have been cut back the previous year soon after it has flowered. I have been even more drastic with *O. macrodonta*, often called the New Zealand holly because of its toothed leaves. This can be very severely pruned and will sprout afresh from old wood.

I find it strange that so little mention is made of *Ribes sanguineum*, the Flowering Currant, as a first-rate seaside shrub, for this common but beautiful, early-flowering shrub stands immovable in the strongest gale, rarely suffers salt-damage or, if it does, it soon recovers. It is also frost-hardy. I have admired it making a most colourful hedge in South Devon close to the sea, and in Kent hedges of it, 5 to 6ft tall, may be seen protecting cherry orchards from the salt winds blowing in over the Thanet coast. One of the best is undoubtedly Pulborough Scarlet, while the dwarf, less vigorous Edward VII has intense crimson flowers. You can prune them to more or less the size you want, cutting out some older wood and shortening younger branches. This is all that is called for to ensure a splendid display of flower the following March. On the mainland of Orkney I came across hedges of *Ribes alpinum* which provided excellent protection against the cruel gales experienced there. The small greenish-yellow flowers were inconspicuous but the dense, close habit of this deciduous shrub offered nearly as much shelter in winter as when in full leaf in summer. The winds in that northern climate prevented it from getting leggy but all it requires is a clipping over in the summer. It is a pity that so few nurserymen stock this useful hedge plant for exposed northern gardens by the sea.

It is a far cry from these northern climes to the hot Mediterranean countries where the ubiquitous goat browses insatiably on the beautiful *Spartium junceum*, and this is a clue to the hard pruning that best suits the Spanish Broom. This valuable shrub for hot, dry situations, with scented golden-yellow flowers, blooms early in summer if pruned in autumn immediately after it has gone out of flower, or it will flower from August until October should pruning be left until the spring. In our seaside garden we cut it hard in early autumn since it carries too much sail to bring it safely through the winter gales. It is almost impossible to prune it too severely as it has wonderful recuperative powers and fresh young growth frequently comes from old wood. The hybrid brooms, however, will not stand this sort of hard treatment, but should have their fresh young growth trimmed back each year after they have flowered in early summer, but never cutting into old wood. Five to six years is their life span and one should start this gentle pruning in infancy.

On the mildest coasts, fuchsias will probably come through all but the severest winters unscathed and make splendid flowering hedges by the sea. Many large-flowered kinds may lose their top growth but will spring up again from the roots. Treat them like hardy perennial plants but retain their top-growth until the spring in frosty districts.

Thus we see it is a fallacy to imagine that any useful purpose is served by a routine annual prune to make all and every shrub flower more freely. Broom, buddleia, weigela, and tree mallow all need annual attention but many shrubs, such as rhododendron, azalea and hydrangea, flower best when left alone, apart from the dead-heading of their flowers.

Page 75: (above)
Eryngium pro-
teiflorum, a Sea Holly;
(below) a self-sown
seedling of the Scotch
Thistle

6

VARIEGATED PLANTS
BESIDE THE SEA

PLANTS whose leaves are variegated are usually a source of controversy, for while many people cannot stand them at any price, some of us cannot resist the lure of leaves gaily splashed or margined with gold or silver. There was a time when any kind of variegation was viewed with suspicion and my own grandfather, a keen plantsman, rarely allowed any plant showing signs of variegation to remain in his garden, as in most cases it was supposed to be an indication of the presence of a virus disease. Nor can I recall any outstanding variegated shrubs in my parents' garden except the hollies and these, resplendent in their green and gold or green and silver dress and decked out with scarlet berries, were very striking.

Be that as it may, many of our best-loved garden plants have variegated forms, particularly in the case of evergreen shrubs which contribute so greatly to the winter scene. It is then, when the eye is not distracted by the bright flowers of summer, that we get their fullest effect. How times have changed and how eagerly many of us now seek them out. The late Margery Fish was a great lover of these plants and many that do well

E

in our seaside garden came from her garden in Somerset. She
once told me she considered that gardeners did not, perhaps,
usually appreciate variegation until they were more experienced
and that she herself had not cared much for them when first
she started gardening. It may be that variegation 'grows'
on gardeners and that the enormous interest now taken by
ardent flower arrangers has stimulated the popularity of
these plants, many of which are strikingly effective in the
home.

To the enthusiast, almost every variegated plant is interesting
but by no means all grow well by the sea and it is unwise to
assume that all those found growing successfully inland will
stand the wear and tear of seaside life. It is worth picking
out the few that withstand direct salt-laden winds on the coast,
and also those others, rather tender ones, which can be very
successful indeed when given shelter, because near the sea they
do not have to contend with the severe frosts of cold inland
gardens.

Where the evergreen *Euonymus japonicus* succeeds in coastal
districts we may safely plant the spectacular *E. j. albo-mar-
ginata*, whose handsome, glossy leaves margined with creamy-
white are so striking at a distance. This makes a rounded bush,
3 to 4ft high. *E. j. aureo-picta* is taller, with bright yellow,
glossy leaves bordered with green. Both may be planted right
on a sandy beach and can be clipped to make bright hedges.
Though slow-growing, they may be moved at any time from
September to May owing to their heavily-fibred root systems.
The creeping *E. fortunei* 'Silver Queen' will brighten a north
wall or can be used as ground cover.

The griselinia is a very wind- and salt-resistant race of evergreens for milder coasts. It will not survive on the cold north-
east coast. In their native New Zealand, *G. littoralis* and *G.
lucida* grow in dense rain forests, often as epiphytes starting
in the forks of trees, as well as in coastal forests and scrub. In

the north of Ireland they are often monumental and seem
able to withstand, with complete equanimity, the periodic
buffetings of the notorious Irish Sea gales, and I know gardens
on the north-west coast of Scotland where they grow beneath
the shade of other trees and the ground beneath is covered
with their seedlings. In the south, it is more often an attractive
shrub of light, apple-green, leathery leaves, usually about 6 to
8ft high, and it is used as an effective wind-sheltering hedge
close to the sea.

The variegated forms are delightful. Three of them show
variegation, *G. littoralis variegata*, *G. lucida variegata* and a
new novelty, *G. littoralis* 'Bantry Bay' that originated on Gar-
nish Island. *G. lucida* is a broad-leaved form of *G. littoralis*,
with much larger, waxy leaves, often 7in long, and it and
G. littoralis shows similar variegation of creamy-yellow margined leaves. The newer *G. l.* 'Bantry Bay' has wavy-margined
leaves with an extensive cream and light green mid-leaf variegation which shows up well at a distance. It is very slow growing but a plant that is bound to attract attention. Griselinias
are happiest on a fairly damp, rich soil and never at their
best on light, sharply-drained sand.

The variegated Elaeagnus, *E. pungens maculata*, must surely
be one of the best known and most widely planted of our
variegated shrubs, but as I have already included it among
my 'star' plants for the seaside garden I will not dwell on its
merits here. Two other brilliantly variegated forms are worth
mention, *E. p. dicksonii*, where the chrome-yellow margins
are broad and irregular and in some leaves cover almost the
entire leaf surface, and *E. p. fredericii*, where the creamy-
yellow occurs in the centre of the leaf, with a broad or narrow
green edge. Either form may produce great variation from
pure green to pure yellow, but when the reversion is entirely
green then the twig concerned should be removed; twigs bearing wholly yellow leaves tend to die out. All these shrubs are

slow growing and cannot be planted too soon to give effect in
the garden.

There is not much doubt that the aucuba, once called the
Spotted Laurel, has made a startling comeback from those
Victorian days when it was used to lighten dank, dark shrub-
beries. Its glossy leaves are as salt-tolerant by the sea as they
are soot-resistant in polluted industrial areas. Both substances
just slide off the highly-polished leaf surfaces. One of the best
of the variegated aucubas is the variety *crotonoides*, whose
broad, glossy leaves are mottled with gold and which bears
large red berries in winter if a male plant is grown nearby.
At one time it was known in England only in its female form
and therefore incapable of bearing fruit, and the male form
of *Aucuba japonica* was first brought to this country from
Japan by Robert Fortune, who evidently thought very highly
of it. 'Only fancy' he wrote 'if all the aucubas which decorate
the windows and squares of our smoky town were covered
during winter and the spring with a profusion of red berries!
Such a result would be worth the journey all the way
from England to Japan.' But in spite of its value as a seaside
plant I cannot like this aucuba, though there is an increasing
demand for it on the Continent, where it is highly esteemed
and where literally thousands of plants are raised each year
for the trade. But there is just one of these shrubs for which
I have an affection, and this is a particularly fine variegated
form, which originated in a Cornish nursery and is called
'Goldenheart'. This is a most gay and attractive shrub, the
centres of whose leaves are all gold with speckled margins,
and if you did not know it was an aucuba I doubt if you would
realise it belonged to such a dull lot of shrubs. Give it a sheltered, shady corner and it will light it up for you. But it is not
as tough as its duller sisters.

I have always been enthusiastic about the golden privet,
Ligustrum ovalifolium aureo-variegatum, in spite of its failure

to do really well on my poor sandy soil. But who can blame it, for there is little here for it and privets are notorious soil-robbers. It will do best in protected seaside gardens or against the house, where it makes a bright clump of pure gold and is a gift for foliage pickers, but never expose it fully to wind and salt or it will lose those lustrous golden leaves to winter gales just when it could be most effective in the flowerless garden. One of the most effective uses I have seen made of it was as beautifully trimmed bushes clothing the white walls of a cottage, where the only other colour in the small garden was that of red roses. Low hedges, clipped with a formal cut twice a year, are excellent for brightening small town gardens in seaside resorts, where other buildings provide the necessary shelter from the saltiest gales. In our garden, we have a pretty form of privet with leaves, grey-green and white, possibly *L. sinense variegatum*, which is far less common than its golden form. It makes a decorative, informal specimen.

One can see the common laurustinus growing wild on Mediterranean coasts. More suprisingly, it thrives close to the sea at Bournemouth and in the Channel Islands. In Jersey, it grows in large bushes where there is sufficient soil, or in interesting dwarf shapes where there is little for it to feed on. It is a most beautiful, winter-flowering shrub, which I feel sure would be more prized if it were not so undemanding. The flat heads of lacy white flowers, opening from pink buds, the reddish stems and the dark green leathery leaves all make the Laurustinus an outstanding seaside shrub for dark winter days. It stands a lot of wind off the sea, yet it is only rarely recommended for seaside planting. *Viburnum tinus* is the name of this sadly neglected shrub which is not fussy about the soil it grows in and ideal for the soils containing lime which are often found close to the sea. This common shrub has a rather tender variegated form with conspicuous yellow markings and distinctly reddish stems. It is not tough enough for full exposure, but its compact habit, slow growth and bright yellow-splashed leaves make it a worthwhile shrub for a sheltered corner in the small modern garden. *V. t. lucidum variegatum* is less common and must have shelter for its large, glossy leaves, lightly touched with creamy-white, but it appreciates the almost frost-free conditions many warm coastal gardens can provide.

For years I grew the hardy *Fatsia japonica*, once *Aralia sieboldii* and often called the False Castor Oil Plant, right on the coast in my Somerset garden, where it was unperturbed by strong gales blowing in from the sea. It is strange that this tall shrub with shining, large green leaves, deeply lobed like those of the ivy to which it is related, and milk-white inflores-cences in branching sprays in autumn, followed by black berry clusters, should stand cliff-top exposure when it is also so good as a house plant. In spite of its exotic and luxuriant appear-ance, it is fully hardy. My variegated form of *Fatsia japonica* has white tips to the leaf lobes and bears similar flowers in October and November, followed by black fruits, but it is more frost-tender. We have it growing in a shady corner be-neath some conifers sheltered from wind. Its shining, seven-point leaves are very popular with flower arrangers, but as it has to be propagated by cuttings it is rather costly to buy.

Among so large a genus of notably wind- and salt-tolerant seaside shrubs as the shrubby hebes from New Zealand, once better known as veronicas, it would surely be surprising if there were not one with good variegation of its leaves. Two are quite outstanding in this respect and readily obtainable, the third is rare and has to be sought out. The charm of the 3 to 4ft tall *H. andersonii variegata* and the dwarfer *H. fran-ciscana (speciosa) variegata* lies mainly in their leaves, though I think the long lavender flower spikes of the former add greatly to the beauty of its large leaves with their distinct cream variegation. It is a pretty shrub for lightening an other-wise dull border. *H. franciscana (speciosa) variegata* has the waxy surface to its leaves that allows the type plant to grow in the most extreme exposure. This splendid maritime shrub is one of the few I found to be totally indifferent to the violent squally gales that sweep over the northern isles. Its variegated form is compact and dwarf, a suitable plant for the small garden, where its brilliant variegation of waxy, creamy-yellow leaves with green mid-ribs and blue flowers can be closely observed. *H. franciscana* 'Tricolor' is a rare, slow growing form, with waxy-textured leaves, grey-green, suffused and margined with creamy-white, and undersurfaces, mid-ribs and margins tinted carmine. This rarity may be seen at the Oxford Botanic Garden, or at Treseders Nurseries, Truro, Cornwall.

Most of us feel the fascination of fuchsias but only occasionally do we come across the delightfully variegated *F. magellanica gracilis versicolor*, a bush some 5ft high with gracefully arching branches of silver-variegated leaves flushed with pink, and small red and purple flowers. I well remember the impact it made on me when first I encountered its frail beauty in the public gardens of a south-coast resort. It needs careful placement, or more robust shrubs, growing nearby, are apt to crowd it out, denying it the sun it needs to bring out its pink, red and rose tints in the growing points. And do not keep it short of water, for fuchsias are greedy drinkers. It will not be killed by frost, and even if cut to ground level during a hard winter it will spring up from the base like an herbaceous perennial plant. Deep planting and a mulch of peat over the roots should see it safely through in colder localities.

Most shrubs with leaves splashed with gold or silver are beautiful in their own right. They are foliage shrubs pure and simple, but the variegated weigela is one that boasts an extra bonus of beautiful flowers. For years relegated to Diervilla, these shrubs have, I am glad to say, now resumed their old and popular name of weigela. So very lovely is the variegation of *W. florida variegata*, a broad bush of golden-edged leaves whose margins take on a pinkish tinge before they drop, that it far surpasses, in my opinion, the type with plain green leaves. In June, the coconut-ice pink flowers are borne in such profusion that the branches bend beneath their weight, but even so the foliage effect remains long after the flowers are gone.

I have never been entirely successful in raising a fine specimen of Buddleia Royal Red Variegata, due perhaps to my rather half-hearted approach to most of the family because their flowers are so short-lived, but *Daphne odora aureomarginata* went straight ahead from cuttings. Reputed to be hardier than the type, it is one of the easiest of sweetly-scented flowering shrubs for the early months of the year. In time, it makes a wide-spreading bush whose every leaf is margined with gold, and the lilac-pink buds open to pinky-white flowers which give off a spicy scent from January to April.

Many rather tender variegated shrubs are mostly hardy in the south and west, but need wall protection elsewhere. Though the pittosporums are too tender for cold areas, where their pretty foliage gets browned and spoilt by frost, they stand a surprising amount of sea wind on our milder coasts. Pittosporums show much variegation and make beautiful small trees in the milder counties. (See Chapter 9.)

The slightly tender *Kerria japonica picta* is a graceful bush that I think gains by its variegation, and when in early summer a bush of silver-margined leaves is spangled with typical single Kerria flowers it makes a pretty sight of silver and gold. The rather uncommon *Coronilla glauca variegata* is completely effective as a foliage plant. It is most attractive as a wall shrub growing up to 4ft and, unlike the type plant, its flowers appear insignificant against leaves heavily variegated with creamy-white. This very tender shrub deserves a warm, sheltered spot away from wind and salt in gardens where frost rarely strikes.

For spiky effect to relieve the monotony of too many flat or rounded shrubs, there is the brightly variegated *Phormium tenax variegata* which I have already included among the 'stars' for a garden at the sea's edge. My own plant of *Phormium colensoi* has pale green, rather lax leaves and tall arching spires of yellow flowers, and is much admired, but there is a variegated form of this handsome plant, *P. colensoi* '*tricolor*', though I have not seen it.

Since I saw and admired a plant of *Yucca filamenosa variegata* in the garden of a friend I have chased this elusive plant without success, for alas, it is not common. You can look through catalogues and not find it there, and when I finally did track it down, it was only to see printed beneath in small letters 'No stock this year'. Variegated plants are often not as effective in flower as their green counterpart, but in the yucca these are every bit as good, and its stiff, glaucous leaves edged with yellow make it attractive at all times.

PERENNIAL PLANTS SHOWING VARIEGATION

If one's love of variegation should extend to perennial plants, then there is a surprising number which, used in the right way, add greatly to the garden scene, particularly where space is too limited for shrubs.

The variegated form of *Vinca major* is one of the most useful plants and no garden is dull where it is grown. I remember a garden on the east coast of Scotland where its only companions were roses, and what a show it made with its bright gold variegated leaves and flowers of true periwinkle blue. Many people grow only the large-leaved periwinkles but there are dwarf and neater kinds with smaller leaves, well suited to the small modern garden, and one of the best of these is the white-flowered form of *V. minor* with a golden variegated leaf. Pulmonarias, 'Soldiers and Sailors' to you and me, have green leaves spotted with white, and *P. saccharata* has flowers of red fading to blue but the leaves are larger and more heavily marked than in *P. officinalis*. This is a good plant for early spring.

One of the most striking plants for a well-drained, sandy soil is a variegated form of *Iris pallida*. Its green and silver, sword-shaped leaves, arranged like a fan, make it a most attractive border plant. Sedums are excellent plants for seaside planting though the pretty variegated form of *S. spectabile*, at its best in shade, needs watching for its tendency to revert to green. Not so the delightfully variegated Phlox 'Norah Leigh', which did not win its award for its rather wishy-washy pink flowers, which I remove so that they do not detract from the beauty of its astonishingly lovely cream and green variegated leaves. Planted in a rich, moist soil, it will create a vivid effect from early June until autumn.

One mint at least found its way into our garden for the sheer beauty of its soft woolly, moss-green leaves. This is *Mentha rotundifolia variegata*, which spreads by means of woody stems just below the surface, to make pretty ground cover. Nor do the sages confine themselves to plain green leaves. They, too, have variegated forms to brighten the garden. The common sage may be good enough for stuffing the duckling but there is a compact, golden variegated form that has never flowered for us, as well as the lovely *Salvia officinalis* 'Tricolor', whose leaves are touched with pink and purple.

Arum maculatum is our native 'Lords and Ladies', but the highly marbled leaves of *A. italicum marmoratum*, which appear in late autumn, are far more showy. The flower arranger loves to pick them to brighten winter flower arrangements indoors, and the fleshy, scarlet berries on prominent heads give a dual season of interest. Another winter brightener is the trailing *Lamium galeobdolon variegatum* the yellow Archangel, whose green leaves look as though painted over with silver. No one need have bare soil with this plant about. It makes a lovely carpet that looks its best in winter when the

silver leaves gleam with startling brilliance. I like it, too, cling-
ing to the branches of some bare shrub, but it needs watching
as it has an irrepressible urge to go on and on for ever.

A bed of variegated honesty in our garden attracted a good
deal of attention in early summer when the combination of
soft mauve flowers and white and green leaves was most effective. Seed of this biennial plant should be sown one year to
flower the next, and self-sown seedlings should occur thereafter
in the garden. Other honesty, *Lunaria annua*, should not be
allowed in the same part of the garden, or should be eliminated
altogether if only variegated ones are wanted.

Even the mini-border can have its variegated plants, though
here they must be real miniatures. From a large plant of the
common arabis with plain green leaves I took a tiny piece that
showed a delightful variegation of green and white, and this
has made a small plant whose leaves display a regular variegation of its leaves. Plants showing variegation are usually less
robust than their greener sisters and this one should not grow
too large for the mini-border. The common London Pride,
Saxifraga umbrosa, has rather gone out of favour but has
returned to my garden in its gold and green form, *S. u. aurea
punctata*. Rather slow-growing, as is often the case with variegated plants, it is very decorative, even when the little pink
flowers are gone. I use it as ground cover for little beds, or it
is good among the roses where is does not intrude. Shade is
usually recommended for London Pride, but I grow it in full
sun where its endearing wee rosettes shine even more golden.

Some weeds should never be discarded. The blue bugle, or
Ajuga reptans to give it its real name, if somewhat invasive,
makes splendid carpeting where its spreading habit is what
is required. So pretty is it that I once won a prize for it at a
local flower show. I try to avoid tracts of bare earth because it
is quite certain they will not remain uncovered for long, but
I did find this plant altogether too much of a spreader and

tried instead *A. reptans variegata*. It is a wee creeper, good on paving stones or for minute patches of ground cover, and there are delightful tiny blue flower spikes as well as pretty leaves, variegated green and white.

For climbers, there are the beautiful ivies. All variegated ivies, large-leaved or small, stand out most magnificently in the winter. *Hedera colchica dentata variegata*, variegated with rich cream, brings sunshine into the darkest corner. I have it growing up the trunk of a pine that has lost its lowest limbs, but it also makes good ground cover in shady places or is outstanding against a white wall. *H. canariensis* 'Gloire de Marengo' has variegation of silver, grey-green with touches of pink, though visitors tell me they are hard put to tell the difference. The small-leaved 'Goldenheart' (Jubilee) has little pointed, dark green leaves with golden centres, and this pretty clinger is scrambling about on an archway above a dark teak door. Cuttings are easy and small rooted pieces are beginning their long ascent up trees in a woody walk.

In winter, one can fully appreciate the golden Japanese Honeysuckle, *Lonicera japonica aureo-reticulata*, when it can be clearly seen flinging out its twining arms to cling to anything within reach. For much of the year its little leaves are netted with gold, but with the colder weather they turn a soft pink. It seldom flowers, it is the leaves that are so attractive. Our other variegated climber is one of the jasmines. Its dainty leaves are margined with creamy-yellow and the long name for this pretty thing is *Jasminum officinale aureo-variegatum*. I would not care if it never flowered, but its pink buds, opening to clusters of white flowers, are similar to those of the type. There is yet another variegated jasmine whose larger leaves are heavily blotched and suffused with gold. This is *J. o. aurem*. Neither is as rampant as the green form and may not prove as hardy.

My latest arrival in the garden is not a climber but is too

good to be omitted altogether. It is a variegated form of *Pachy-sandra terminalis*, which in its green counterpart has plain green leaves but in 'variegata' the leaves are broad-banded with silver. The small greenish flowers are of no importance but it is a valuable prostrate plant that does not exceed 8in in height but will spread indefinitely in a shady place. Since childhood, when the small sky-blue forget-me-not flowers and huge green leaves of a plant then known as *Anchusa myosotidi-flora* grew in abundance along the edge of a stream in my parents' garden, this has been a favourite of mine, but now a gay variegated form of it has assumed the name of *Brunnera macrophylla 'Variegata'*, which does nothing to describe it but should not deter people from growing this useful and long-lived hardy perennial plant.

Though botanical gardens are ideal places in which to study all such plants at one time, and there is a goodly collection at the Oxford Botanical Gardens, I doubt if this sort of shoulder to shoulder planting of plants whose foliage is variegated appeals to the amateur gardener, nor does it show off the plants themselves to their best advantage. 'Enough is enough' and one can have too much of a good thing. The way to grow these plants is as single specimens, or in groups of one kind to brighten plain or dark-leaved plants, with a special eye to the winter scene, when the variegated shrubs gleam like lamps in the darkness, simulate sunshine and are definite scene-stealers. Often then they are the brightest gems in the whole garden. We spend a great deal of our time looking out of our windows during the dullest days of the year, and nothing is more glad-dening on a dreary day than to gaze upon some gold or sil-vered bush we planted with just this pleasure in mind.

TENDER PLANTS
FOR WARM GARDENS

ONE of the strangest things about gardening is how little the average gardener taps the vast wealth of material at his disposal. He would rather grow something he sees flourishing in his neighbour's garden than experiment with anything new. This, of course, is understandable since there is no risk attached, but it makes for a sameness in gardens which can be monotonous. In an age when a general levelling and standardisation is the order of the day, many people like to set their sights a little higher and gardening provides us with just this opportunity.

Someone once said 'A tender plant is one that looks too good to be true and usually proves it'. This may well be so, but meanwhile what pleasure there is in growing a plant known to be too tender for cold, frosty districts inland, but which, when carefully sited in a warmer garden by the sea, comes through all but the worst winters unharmed.

When I suggest some of the beautiful and unusual plants asking to be grown, the answer invariably is the same : 'If I were a rich man'. And admittedly it is a gamble with plants of doubtful hardiness, many of which come from countries hotter than our own and which gardening books recommend for the cool greenhouse. Indeed, gardeners who, like myself, suffered the ill effects from hard frost, heavy snow and arctic easterly winds as recently as 1969, may be forgiven if they are deterred from experimenting further, but it should be remembered that for six years, since the abnormal winter of 1963, many tender plants have given infinite pleasure to the owners. It is fortunate, too, that many tender plants are rapid growers, and if seedlings or rooted cuttings are kept ready in frame or greenhouse, replacements will be there for replanting when necessary.

NEVER WASTE THE HOUSE WALLS

House walls are the most precious places in the whole garden, whether open to sunshine or in shade. It is surprising how the microclimate varies in the few inches closest to a solid wall and provides ideal situations for borderline plants unfitted for the rigours of the open garden. We who live by the sea, with more freedom from frost than further inland, should particularly prize our house walls, some of which give almost subtropical conditions. Against these walls the soil will certainly be the driest and possibly the poorest in the whole garden. Special attention will need to be paid to watering and in some cases to feeding, though when we are considering the controversial subject of the hardiness of plants, good drainage is a potent factor. A plant that will come through straight frost on a light, sharply-drained soil will not survive if its roots have to endure water-logged conditions.

I feel that any gardener with house walls to clothe should not content himself with hardy plants which he knows will flourish in the open, but should experiment with some exciting plant known to be a little tender but which can be so rewarding when it succeeds. It may succeed for perhaps seven or

eight years and then be killed by one of our periodical severe
winters of hard frost and killing winds—and I say killing winds
advisedly because, on the coast, wind plus frost causes more
damage than straight frost alone. Often a heavy mulch over the
roots of a tender plant brings it safely through cold weather.
On the other hand, very many tender plants will live for years,
and though they look forlorn and miserable after a hard spell,
new growth appears with the coming of spring and all is well
again.

The Passion Flower, *Passiflora caerulea*, is such a plant. It
may get blasted by icy winter gales, yet by May it will be
coming into strong growth, not only from lower down but
from points far up the stem. When selecting a site for it, it
should be remembered that it is a rampant grower, climbing
by means of tendrils, and because it is a native of Central and
South America it revels in warmth. Given a south- or west-
facing wall, it will keep up a long succession of its strange
symbolic flowers of creamy petals and blue filaments from
July until frost strikes, and the orange fruits that follow after
a hot summer are as ornamental as the flowers. It is not fussy
as to soil, and I have seen it flowering well in a large pot where
its root run was curtailed. Often it may fail to flower if it has
had too lush a diet or is planted in shade, but give it meagre
rations and a place in the sun and its beauty will astonish you.
There is, too, a delightful white form, Constance Elliot, which
shows up well against a red brick wall, and the lilac-pink
P. x. tresederi 'Lilac Lady' would be worth a trial where conditions were specially favourable.

Anyone with a warm south or west wall waiting to be clothed
should consider the Trumpet Vine; perhaps the hardiest is
Campsis radicans 'Mme Galen', climbing to 15ft in time, with
long, scarlet and orange trumpets in late summer and early
autumn, at a time when most wall plants are past their best.
For a really hot, sunny wall there is no more exciting pea

Page 93: (left) Phormium tenax variegatum; (right) Olearia scilloniensis

Page 94 : (above) Griselinia littoralis variegata; (below) Fatsia japonica

flower than the tender scarlet or white-flowered *Clianthus puniceus*, known as the Lobster Claw or Parrot's Bill because of its curious long keels. Spread a mulch of peat around its roots in winter and add some snail deterrent, for this is a delicacy snails cannot resist. A similar protection for its roots is also essential to bring the tender *Cassia corymbosa* through a hard winter, and in a garden by the sea where I admired it covering a high wall with its vivid, glossy, pinnate foliage, reminiscent of laburnum, and clusters of large flowers of the richest gold, I was told that it liked a blanket over its roots during the winter months. This must be a plant easily propagated from seed, since the nearby greenhouse was filled with a number of small seedling plants.

As a late-summer flowering plant, *Phygelius capensis coccineus* is invaluable. Though in some gardens I have seen this native of the Cape grown as a shrub in the open garden, it is of doubtful hardiness but makes a splendid wall plant where its coral-red flowers will show to advantage. A correspondent from the Essex coast writes that on her house, which faces south-east and catches the full force of the cold winds that blow in from the Continent, it came through an arctic winter successfully. There it reached 5ft against a wall, but in more sheltered parts of the country it would grow much taller.

Garrya elliptica is one of the finest subjects for that cold north wall, and in January and February it presents a remarkable appearance with its long catkins, longer in the male plant than in the female. I have been growing on a north wall in our garden on the north coast of Cornwall a distinctive form, *G. e. James Roof*, from California. Not reputed to be as tough as the type, it has made very sturdy growth in two years and in its third year I am looking forward to its immensely long and decorative tassels. There is another garrya hybrid—not yet named, though it has gained an Award of Merit—which is the result of a cross between *G. fremontii* and the well-known

F

G. elliptica. Its foliage is similar to the latter but the 4in long catkins are banded with deep pink and green and the stems are reddish. If it proves as hardy as *G. elliptica* it will indeed be a find.

The Chilean Potato Tree, *Solanum crispum,* is a very vigorous wall plant, and the form Glasnevin, or *autumale,* is more free of its flowers and continues in flower over a longer period than the species. On a south-facing wall, where it has the support of a plastic-covered trellis but is exposed to south-westerly gales off the sea, it never fails to flower for us from May until September, with sprays of purple-blue 'potato' flowers with golden centres. In spring, we cut it hard back against the wall. This is a plant very easy to propagate from cuttings in a frame, and once planted it grows very fast indeed.

Not so long ago, I was given a plant of the very beautiful but tender *Lapageria rosea* from a garden where it covered a high wall. Unfortunately it does need a peaty, lime-free soil and was not one for my hot, sunny garden and my limy sand. This is one of the loveliest twiners I know, with evergreen leaves and long, bell-like flowers looking as though fashioned in shining rose-pink wax. Where soil and conditions are right it is well worth a gamble for so rewarding a plant as this. It does not care for direct sunshine, but is just the thing for a courtyard whose walls give it the amount of shade it much prefers.

Fremontia californica, on the other hand, likes all the sun it can get and a hot, sharply-drained soil on the poor side. Given these, it will bear the most beautiful open, butter-cup yellow flowers with remarkably protruding stamens through-out the summer, set off by unusually attractive, heart-shaped leaves, olive green above and rusty-brown with hairs beneath. Though I have known it as a bush in the open garden, I much prefer it roughly trained in the shape of a fan against a sunny wall. I have found rooting cuttings difficult, though it is easy

to grow from seed sown in spring in a warm greenhouse, preferably in peat pots so that there is no disturbance of the roots
when planting it into the garden. The best results may be expected during a really hot summer—all too rare in England.

The very beautiful *Teucrium fruticans azureum*, brought
from the Atlas Mountains by Collingwood Ingram, has flowers
of the softest blue. It, too, likes a position on a sunny wall,
and in the open only comes through the winter in mild sheltered gardens. This delightful shrub has a greener and slen-
derer growth than that of the hardier *Teucrium fruticans*
which is one of the best grey-leaved shrubs on the coast and
whose pale lavender flowers, white stems and grey leaves with
white undersides stand up so surprisingly well to exposed situations by the sea.

A few of the beautiful evergreen Mutisias from South
America are only more or less hardy in the milder parts of
our island, and then against walls or in sheltered positions
under over-hanging trees. *M. oligodon*, from Chile, has leaves
shining green above and woolly underneath and, in summer,
satiny pink daisy flowers which have earned it the title of
'Climbing Gazania', which it closely resembles. It climbs by
means of tendrils and will ramble through another shrub as
host, up a tree, or, less well perhaps unless it is helped up a
trellis, against a wall. The best site for this beautiful plant is
on a rich, well-drained soil from which it can climb into sunshine while its lower parts remain in the shade. Plant during
October, or in March or April, and protect the young plants
from slugs by placing cinders and a proprietary slug-killer
around the base. Though it received an Award of Merit as
long ago as 1928, it is only rarely seen in gardens.

An intriguing wall plant that never fails to excite attention,
if not always much admiration, is *A. megapotamicum*, not
strictly a climber but easily satisfied on wire or trellis against
a low wall. Dark crimson and yellow flowers, like small lan-

terns with bell-hangers of pronounced brownish stamens, hang down from the slender branches of this, for my part, charming and unusual plant. It will flower all summer, and even up to Christmas if given a warm, sunny wall out of the wind.

I am doubtful if *Mimulus glutinosus*, the Californian 'Shrubby Mimulus', really needs the shelter of a wall, though this is the position in which I have most often seen this tender plant. It is an exceedingly pretty 4ft shrub for mild districts, especially by the sea, with sticky leaves and large buff or salmon-yellow flowers, similar in shape to those of the well-known Monkey Musk, *M. luteus*. In 'puniceus', the flowers are crimson-scarlet. This is another plant which, though it received its Award of Merit as long ago as 1938, is not often seen in gardens.

PLANTS ON THE BORDERLINE OF HARDINESS FOR THE OPEN GARDEN

'Is it hardy?' is a question I am often asked, but the weather in Britain is so unpredictable that no sooner has a plant earned a reputation for hardiness than we are proved wrong by some unforeseen freak of Nature. These plants I have in mind are only hardy *some* of the time and in *some* gardens, but there is not one of them I have not known at some time or other looking beautiful in some garden by the sea.

Though *Buddleia colvelei* is most often found growing against a wall, constant pruning to keep it under control will have diminished the production of its beautiful panicles of rose-coloured flowers, so to avoid having the prune it, try it instead in a sheltered sunny corner of the garden and note the difference.

There are two forms of the lovely *Abutilon vitifolium*, one with wide-open, pale lavender flowers the colour of parma violets, and the other, just as beautiful, pure white with conspicuous golden stamens. You can take your choice, and either is well worth having. An ideal situation for these delightful, tall shrubs is against a dark background, where their soft vine-like leaves, white stems and appealing open flowers show to perfection. How unfortunate it is that they are not longer lived. For no apparent reason, a bush that appears in the prime of life abruptly dies. Such a loss occurred recently in our garden. It was not frost that killed it, for it died during a par-ticularly mild winter. Had it exhausted the soil? There seems no valid reason for their sudden demise and we simply have to accept that these abutilons are not long lived. Fortunately, Nature has seen to it that they often perpetuate themselves by self-sown seedlings around the parent plant, and seed sown in a cold greenhouse will germinate like mustard and cress. Thus replacements are easy, and the abutilon grows very fast indeed.

Hybrid abutilons, such as Kentish Belle, deep orange, Ash-ford Red, salmon-red, Louis Marignac, pink, Boule de Neige, white, and Canary Bird, pale yellow, flower almost non-stop in a cool greenhouse, and I have a fine plant with soft maple leaves and pale yellow cups beside me as I write. I have tried them in the open garden but without much success, their flowering has been brief and spasmodic. The finest specimens I have ever seen were in the National Trust Garden, Sharpitor, at Salcombe, where 'Ashford Red' and 'Canary Bird' flowered in great profusion against a high wall on either side of the garden door, the red seeming to vie with its yellow companion in the abundance of their flowers. When grown in pots or containers they flower freely, and their hanging bells make pretty additions to patio or paved terrace, or they are decora-tive plants for the modern sunroom.

Many exciting shrubs from Australia are frost-tender but I have come across the grevilleas in quite unexpected places in this country. They seem to me to like a light, free-draining soil, the sort of soil where rosemary and cistus do well. Indeed

G. rosmarinifolia is named after the rosemary for its distinct rosemary-like foliage. Though it is not often mentioned as a winter-flowering shrub, the strange, spidery, red flowers begin to flower in winter and though a 4ft bush makes no bright patch of colour, gardeners appear to find its very unusualness intriguing. *G. sulphurea* bears a distinct resemblance to a golden conifer, and with its pale, golden-yellow flowers and foliage tinged with gold it looks its best against a background of shrubs with darker leaves. It is more robust than *G. rosmarinifolia*, often reaching 6ft high with an equally wide spread. The shrubby *Calceolaria integrifolia* is very gay from June until autumn, with clusters of bright yellow flowers, pouched in the way we have come to associate with calceolarias. It likes a good, rich soil and a place in the sun.

One is always on the lookout for plants to carry on the flowering season late in the year, and it was late September when I first encountered *Leonotis leonorus*, the South African Lion's Tail. You will not see it in many gardens, since most gardening books recommend it for the cool greenhouse, though it is hardy enough in mild localities and the conspicuous whorls of downy, orange flowers on erect stems carry on into October. The tender *Lespedeza thunbergii* is another late flowerer, a leguminous plant with clover-like leaves that have given it the name of Bush Clover. A 4ft bush carries racemes of rose-purple pea-flowers on long, pendulous shoots and so prolific is its flowering that the shoots bend visibly under their weight. In flower at the same time as the Spanish Broom, when the latter is pruned in spring, the effect when grown together is striking and unusual. In spring, the shoots should be hard pruned. To complete the trio of late flowerers there is the Mexican Incense Bush, *Eupatorium micranthum*, an attractive, rounded bush of dark green leaves and pinky-white flat heads of flower, rather reminiscent of the gysophila, on long stalks that make them useful as cut flowers. They have a pleasant scent and butterflies flock to them as they do to sedum or buddleia.

Shrubs with a long flowering season are always welcome. The shrubby milkwort, *Polygala myrtifolia*, carries its magenta-purple flowers with a white brush of anthers from spring until autumn, and though it is frost-tender I have known it make a large bush, 3ft through, in an exposed position on the coast. It is easily increased from cuttings in a frame. I have not been so fortunate with rooting cuttings of the evergreen laburnum, *Piptanthus laburnifolius*, once known as *P. nepalensis*, though it sets quantities of seed from which it may be grown. In a cold climate it may lose its leaves in winter, though in many a coastal garden it is evergreen or almost so. A height of 8 to 10ft is the average for this Himalayan shrub, and against a wall a little more. The bright-yellow, pea-shaped flowers are borne in clusters during May and June, not in long trails like those of the laburnum but in short, erect spikes. It detests disturbance of its roots at any time and is best sown in individual peat pots which may be planted intact into the ground.

All too few nuserymen stock the very handsome *Pachystegia insignis*, though you may find it listed in catalogues under *Olearia insignis*. It is the same half-hardy shrub from the north of South Island in New Zealand, a low-growing shrub wider than it is tall and distinguished by the most beautiful leathery, grey leaves, often 7in long, with white underfelt.. The flower-heads are white with yellow central discs and appear in August, carried singly on stiff, downy, white stalks with a white tomentum, though it is the leaves that I find so attractive. It is a first-class low shrub for maritime gardens, thriving in hot, dry places. It is a pity it is so rarely seen as it could be a most welcome addition to any garden which was not too cold for it. And if the demand were greater, nurserymen would no doubt be more willing to stock these half-hardy plants.

At one time I grew *Sparmannia africanus* in a cool green-

house until it threatened to have the roof off. We moved it to
the open garden to a very dry situation under some conifers
where it flourished for many years, and its great soft, green
leaves and white flowers with a central brush of red and yellow
in early spring surprised visitors by the luxuriance with which
it grew in such unlikely surroundings. It used to be a favourite
pot-plant in Victorian conservatories and, like so many of
these, is much tougher than was supposed. The bitter winter of
1969 appeared to have killed it and we had it out, but my
husband, who is a confirmed optimist, put its stump and roots
into a large pot and left it in the garden to look after itself. To
my amazement, he produced it a few months later to show
me that it was putting out a few leaves from the stump. We
have now replanted it in its original position where it is doing
well—an extraordinary revival for so supposedly tender a
plant.

Usually *Hedychium gardnerianum*, the Ginger Lily, is looked
upon as a plant to be grown under glass, though it grows in
many gardens within the sea's influence and has proved hardy
once it has established itself. In one garden I visited it made
a large patch about 6 to 8ft across between the buttresses of
a wall, where it had survived many hard winters, including
the severe one of 1947 when the sea froze at its edges. In yet
another garden, plants of *H. gardnerianum* had been in one
position for over forty years. They were growing against the
east-facing wall of a cold greenhouse and had received no
treatment of any kind during that time. The huge, canna-
like leaves of this handsome Indian plant are often cut down
in winter, but soon the spikes of the leaves re-appear above
ground and in summer the fine heads of fragrant lemon-yellow
flowers are really lovely. One spike of flower will scent a whole
house. The RHS *Dictionary of Gardening*, speaking of hedy-
chiums, says 'Several are nearly hardy and will, in favoured
conditions, stand the winter on a south border with a little

protection', and later it refers to *H. gardnerianum* as one of the hardiest. I feel that a plant such as this, that came through winters like 1947 and 1963, when many eucalypts in the area died, is worth a gamble. I am growing it at first under glass and when it is sufficiently large I shall plant it in the garden.

Clumps of *Phormium tenax*, the New Zealand Flax, can be seen buffeted by gales and soused with salt spray in many gardens at the sea's edge. In coastal gardens on the western seaboard of Scotland, it is largely used as protection for other plants, but *P. tenax purpureum*, shining with bronze-purple leaves, is only rarely seen. This more uncommon plant is no tough, wind-sheltering plant but a more tender one, whose rich purple colouring makes a splendid contrast for plants with gold or silver foliage. It likes moist, rich soil, plenty of sun and freedom from wind.

Falmouth, like many other south-west seaside resorts, is famous for its semi-tropical dracaena palms, *Cordyline australis*. They grow along the roadside, in private gardens as well as in public parks; indeed Dracaena Avenue, Falmouth's broad, tree-lined approach to the town, takes its name from these exotic trees. They are a feature of seaside resorts not only in the south but also in the Isle of Man and places further north within the sea's influence. I am not a lover of these New Zealand Cabbage Palms when left untended, for no plant, in my opinion, looks more moth-eaten than a cordyline when it has been damaged by frost. Some few seem to drop their leaves and look much more as Nature must have intended them to be. Only rarely do they flower with such profusion as in 1969, when trees in Falmouth were covered with such masses of creamy-white mopheads of flowers and the air was so heavy with their scent that they were blamed for the running eyes and sneezing that affected many summer visitors. The cordyline has remarkable powers of recovery and often bursts into leaf

again after quite a hard frost. The stout vertical trunk is un-
moved by the strongest gale.

What a triumph if you could grow a metrosideros, perhaps
M. lucida, well-named from the Greek *metra*, the heart or
middle, and *sideros*, iron, in reference to the toughness of its
wood. Though frost-tender, it is wonderfully wind-tolerant
and will withstand sea breezes and salt spray readily enough.
This is the southern rata of New Zealand, with polished myrtle-
like leaves and flowers of the brightest crimson in July. Fine
specimens may be seen in the Abbey Gardens, Tresco, in the
Isles of Scilly, and in other warm maritime districts. Plant
from pots, or try it out in your garden in its pot for the first
year to acclimatise it to your conditions. If you have a warm,
sheltered garden, you might try an oleander. *Nerium odorum*,
the Indian Oleander, is reputed to be less frost-tender than
the Mediterranean one, and has dark or pale pink flower clusters from mid-summer onwards. There are also good double
forms. Oleanders will tolerate prolonged periods without water
but appreciate an occasional feed during the summer. Prune
the flower stalks hard back after flowering. A word of warning
about the oleanders. Their foliage and their flowers are extremely poisonous to animals and children and have been
known to cause deaths. Hands should be washed in soapy
water before handling food.

If *Fascicularia pitcairnifolia*, sometimes called Ben's Pineapple, though I have yet to discover why, and still listed in
some nurserymen's catalogues as *Rhodostachys pitcairnifolia*,
were not doubtfully tender I might have included it among
the 'stars'. My own plant, grown in shade, did nothing for
me until it was moved into a warmer, sunnier situation facing
south, when it at once showed how much it had disliked its
previous rather gloomy position by putting out more of its
long, curving shoots that carry the narrow, barbed leaves,
paler beneath than above. The whole plant to me rather sug-

gests a huge sea anemone, with immense rosettes of down-turning, prickly shoots with stemless, blue flowers nestling in a bright red centre. When first I came across it flowering in a garden by the sea I thought it looked like something from outer space. In fact it comes from Chile, and though it has not yet flowered for me it has survived a couple of hard winters and I am looking forward to its strange exotic flowers in early autumn.

I shall never forget my first sight one June of some lepto-spernums against a blue sea, where their arching, twiggy branches and small, thyme-like leaves were lost beneath a mass of rich, rosy-crimson, myrtle-like flowers. It was a variety 'Nichollsii' of *L. scoparium*, the Manuka or Tea Tree, said to have been found on the sandhills north of Christchurch in New Zealand. Leptospernums grow best on a well-drained sandy soil free from lime. They are not really hardy in the British Isles, though they may be seen in milder maritime districts beautifying gardens in Ireland, on the western seaboard of Scotland and near the sea in Cornwall. Other very attractive kinds are the double-flowered 'Red Damask', very long-lasting in flower and probably as hardy as 'Nichollsii', and the deep carmine-pink 'Rowland Bryce'. It is not surprising that leptospernums appreciate sea air since one species, *L. laevigatum*, is called the Coastal Tree and is abundant along the east coast of Australia. A dense-foliaged tall shrub whose small leaves are very wind- and salt-resistant, it is reputed to have few equals as a sand binder, and will stand where no other tree will. Most garden hybrids have developed from this plant.

HALF-HARDY PERENNIAL PLANTS

There are many half-hardy perennial plants which will come through any normal winter in some coastal garden. The trouble with a lot of them is that they are too often recommended for pot culture or for the cool greenhouse, so that seaside gardeners who could grow them outside take fright. But nurserymen have to take these precautions on their own account, or customers would expect replacements should they die. No one tells us that they are worth the risk of growing them outdoors in warm localities, or how easily they may be grown from seed or cuttings so that any losses during a particularly severe winter can be readily replaced. If we are not careful in this age of standardisation we may lose some of these borderline plants from our gardens in Britain, and we shall have to go abroad to see them in their native South Africa or in Mediterranean regions.

Though the common bindweed is such a pest in gardens, some of its exotic relations are delightful garden plants and, far from being a nuisance, are cherished in our anxiety to keep them alive. This is very true of the beautiful *Convolvulus mauritanicus*. My own lasting remembrance of this enchanting trailing plant was cascading down from a rocky ledge in the cliff gardens of St Michael's Mount, where its soft mauve-blue open flowers, resembling a convolvulus, grew in such profusion that the mass of flower vied with the blue sea beneath. The rather tender *C. althaeoides* is another sprawler, with flowers of the softest pink, only invasive in very warm maritime districts where it is entirely at home. Either plant is easy to grow from cuttings.

Nor is the pretty, sun-loving blue marguerite, *Felicia amelloides*, sometimes known as *Agathaea coelestis*, reliably hardy. In many gardens in the milder parts of New Zealand it is as common as geraniums. But who, once having grown this small bushlet of sky-blue daisies with yellow centres, would wish to be without its all-summer flowering? Seed provides the easiest means of increase in a slightly heated greenhouse very early in the spring.

A specially bitter winter put paid to my gazanias except the hardier, prostrate *G. splendens*. This was a severe blow until I found that seed, sown in slight heat in March, produced plants that flowered the same year, and from these plants cuttings could be taken to perpetuate the loveliest. May is the month for planting out the half-hardy perennial gazanias, and there is nothing to be gained by too early planting. They give a dazzling display of colour when the sun shines, and obviously are at their gayest during a hot summer. They are not reliably frost-hardy—in cold inland gardens they will not survive— though the dwarf, spreading *G. splendens*, with black central zone surrounded by a fringe of orange petals, has come through some very sharp winters on our paved terrace on the north coast of Cornwall.

Gazanias are not all prostrate by any means; many top a foot in height and these have some of the loveliest combinations of colour to be found in the plant world. Few flowers have so brilliant a variation of colours—cream, dead white, yellow, pink, tangerine and darkest flame—and that is not all, for not many flowers can boast a central zone of emerald green surrounded by a fringe of pink petals or a pale green disk edged by petals of the palest citron-yellow. The leaves, too, show variation, some being green with silver lining, others altogether silver-grey. Gazanias are the Treasure Flowers of South Africa, and its sun-drenched veldt gives us a clue to the sort of hot conditions they prefer, but it is a fallacy to assume, as people often do, that their daisy flowers only open as long as the sun is shining, for I have found that they open up when the temperature is warm enough, even if the sun is shrouded by clouds. And though they like a sunny situation they seem, at least in this country, to like an occasional watering during drought conditions.

The Dimorphothecas, Stars of the Veldt, have much in common with the gazanias; they, too, hail from South Africa, close their petals when the sun sets and, apart from

one species, are not reliably frost-hardy. *D. barberiae*, with
lilac-pink daisies with yellow centres rising from a mass of
aromatic herbage, is much hardier than is generally supposed
and usually survives outdoors in the south of England and in
maritime areas further north. It is the Cinderella of the family,
and since it stands many degrees of frost and is impervious to
salt spray drifting in from the sea it is the one most often seen
in seaside gardens, though by no means the most beautiful. Its
spreading habit may be curtailed by cutting it hard back in
the spring, but for small gardens the more compact form,
D. b. compacta, is a better plant. Next in hardiness I place
'Wisley Hybrid', a neat mat, with flowers of a dazzling purity
contrasting with a dark blue centre, and since it rarely occupies
more than a foot across it is most suited to a garden with little
space.

  D. ecklonis can get rather out of hand, since, even from a
rooted cutting, it takes up a good deal of room in its first
summer, but it is a most attractive member of the family
with large, slender-stemmed daisies of icy whiteness with a
contrasting central zone of dark blue and gold. The beautiful
D. hybrida rosea is slightly hardier, with the loveliest combination of satiny pink petals surrounding a bright blue central
disk, and rarely escapes notice in any garden. The firm stems
of these two make them excellent cut flowers, though it should
be remembered that they will close their petals by evening.
This, however, is not so important with the newer 'Blue
Streak', a form with bright blue streaks along the reverse side
of its petals, which are very prominent when the flowers close
at night, reminding one of a piece of candy-striped material.
During the day it makes an erect bushy plant with a succession
of dazzling white daisy flowers with dark blue centres.

  Two trailers are useful for hanging from a rocky crevice,
or draping a sunny wall. Neither is very hardy. The white
petals of *D. jucunda* are heavily backed with blue-purple in

the bud stage and when the flowers close, and the central disk is an equally dark purple colour, so that a hanging plant makes a striking picture against a sunny wall. The wine-pink *D. jucunda rosea* has a similar trailing habit. It is necessary to perpetuate the dimorphothecas by cuttings since they will not stand sharp frost or killing easterly winds, but they root very easily in a frame in late summer and quickly make good flowering plants if planted out in May.

8

THE FASCINATION
OF SMALL THINGS

WITH labour neither cheap nor plentiful, a high premium on building land and a widespread policy of 'in-filling', it is not surprising that new gardens are becoming smaller all the time. And nowhere is this more apparent than on the coast, where there is increasing demand for miniscule plots of land on which to build holiday houses or homes for retirement. Seaside homes are no longer the prerogative of the elderly, and people much younger than those traditionally associated with cottages by the sea are now buyers in a restricted market. The motor-car has changed everything.

As these seaside plots rarely exceed a quarter or half an acre, their maintenance is within the scope of the 'do-it-yourself' gardener on short holidays, or of the retired owner who is averse to saddling himself with more than he can manage. But it is one thing to make a lovely garden with a good deal of ground at one's disposal, and quite another to transform a small plot into a garden that will give pleasure to its owners and to those who visit it.

The size of a garden is irrelevant. That great gardener, Gertrude Jekyll, said 'The size of a garden has little to do

Page 111: (above) *Hedychium gardnerianum*, the Ginger Lily; (below) *Mutisia oligodon*, the Climbing Gazania

Page 112: (above) *Euphorbia epithymoides,* a small spurge with yellow bracts; (below) *Dimorphotheca hybrida rosea*

with its merit. It is merely an accident relating to the circum-
stances of the owner'. I have seen the loveliest subjects in
pocket-sized gardens, where many a plant that would be passed
over in a vast estate receives its due meed of admiration.

Unfortunately, small gardens close to the sea constitute a
special challenge. They get wind straight off the sea, the salt,
and often their quota of sand as well, blown in from nearby
sand dunes or a sandy beach. They are often too narrow and
confined to allow of any attempt at providing a shelter belt
of vegetation, and there may not even be room for the most
wind-tolerant shrubs. The answer then is some sort of artificial
screening which, even if only 3ft high, will wiffle the wind,
lifting it up and over the garden for eight times the height of
the fence. Such screening does not occupy as much room as
a hedge of living material, nor does it rob the precious soil.
There is no need to fence in the entire garden, merely to site
some fencing to protect the garden from the worst winds.

Small gardens very easily become too complicated. Owners
who are collectors—and I have much sympathy with them—
want to cram as many plants as possible into the tiny space
available. Nothing, I know, will stop the dedicated plantsman,
but too many eye-catching plants in a limited space vie with
one another to the detriment of all. It is better, *if* one can,
to ask oneself 'Where can I put it? Will it really go in my
garden?' This is not easy, but it is the most practical method
in the long run. In small gardens each plant has to count and
for as long as possible. The great thing is to keep a critical eye
and a questioning mind before acquiring a new plant. Should
your garden be really minute, then forgo the brightest colours.
I know this is hard to do when we are all trying to brighten
our rather drab lives, but the pocket-sized plot appears even
smaller if only highly-coloured plants are grown. Go for pastel
shades and plants with grey foliage and the garden will appear
larger than it actually is. Pastel shades show up well in an

G

evening light and many see their gardens only at this time
or at week-ends. Restrict the range of plants and repeat these;
it is a good idea to plant three of a kind instead of one. Plants
by the sea like this sort of planting, it gives wonderful comfort
to them in exposed places and improves the effect of the garden
as a whole.

POCKET-SIZED SHRUBS

For gardens where space is limited, look for pocket-sized
editions of well-known maritime plants. Their number may
be limited but so is the space they are required to fill. Many
of the best shrubs for seaside planting have their miniatures,
shrublets that never grow to more than 3ft in height or take
years to reach it. They are distinguished in catalogues by
adjectives such as *nana*, *microphylla* or *pumila*. Though even
here there is need for care, for I have known *Cortaderia argentea pumila*, reputedly a dwarf form of Pampas-grass, reach 6ft.

The berberis family have excellent miniatures, suitable for
any soil in sun or shade, and they do well by the sea. *B. darwinii nana*, or *prostrata* is a small replica of the well-known,
tall *B. darwinii*, with similar bright orange flowers in spring, *B.
stenophylla gracilis nana* is a small globular shrub smothered
early in the year with tiny yellow flowers, and *B. thunbergii
atropurpurea nana* is charming with purplish-red leaves all
summer. They associate well with that minutest of all santolinas, *S. incana* 'Weston', whose leaf is whiter and woollier
than *S. incana*. No garden is too miniscule for this midget.
Though in inland gardens the artemisias do need a little coddling
to bring them through the winter, they are happier on the
coast when not subjected to severe frost, and their very finely
dissected foliage, which is so attractive, should never be cut
down in winter in the interests of tidiness. Spring is the time
to cut them over, just before they are putting on fresh growth.
A. schmidtii nana is a little grey mound of ferny, filigree foliage.

Many hypericums recommended in gardening books are far too large for a small patch, but *H. polyphyllum* is just the thing, a beautiful sub-shrubby plant, never higher than 12in, massed with tufts of erect stems bearing buds tinged with scarlet and opening to large, deep yellow flowers from July onwards. Not to be confused with the madly invasive *H. calycinum*, it is compact and knows its place. Like the hypericums, potentillas have a very long flowering season from May until frost. They vary in size, but from the low-growing ones I single out *P. beesii*, a silvery mass about 18in high, studded with yellow flowers. *P. arbuscula* is a most desirable dwarf plant with a spreading habit and large canary-yellow saucers. Hypericums and potentillas are excellent shrubs for northern coastal gardens, where they are appreciated for their toughness in the face of cold winds blowing in from the sea. It was on the mainland of Orkney that I came across a minute willow, *Salix lanata*, an enchanting small bushlet around 2ft high, with silvery leaves coated with silky hairs and small branches clothed in soft grey wool. In May, tiny catkins hang on the branches, making a pretty picture of silver and gold. It did not survive in our garden on the Cornish coast, preferring its native habitat of high altitudes.

Cotoneasters are so tough that they will grow anywhere, north or south, and are excellent plants for dry, limy soils where they seed themselves. They tolerate extreme exposure and the little *C. microphylla* may be seen hugging the ground or moulding itself round a boulder at the sea's edge. This semi-prostrate shrub has smaller, darker leaves than *C. horizontalis* and sparser but larger berries.

We do not grow the spiraeas nearly enough in seaside gardens. Many are altogether too large for small gardens but *S. japonica alpina* is an attractive dwarf, a low cushion of grey foliage and flowers of warm rose-pink. *S. bullata* is even more of a dwarf, seldom exceeding a mere 18in with flat crimson heads of flower. The trouble with most lilacs is that they take up a great deal of room and are no ornament to the garden when out of flower, but *Syringa palibiniana*, literally smothered during May with pinkish-mauve flowers that scent the garden, will not be much more than 3 to 4ft tall after ten years. In nurserymen's catalogues you may find it under *S. velutina* or *S. microphylla*, but it is the same plant.

Owners of small gardens will wish to take advantage of any scheme that gives concentrated and economical use of their limited space, and one giving two seasons of flower is particularly satisfactory. An idea that appealed to me was one I saw carried out in a very small garden in Aberdeen, where a few bushes of the grey-leaved *Buddleia fallowiana* 'Lochinch' were planted at regular intervals down a short path leading to the front door of the house. Each was grown in semi-standard form, with a short main stem from which all side shoots had been removed, with a bushy top of silvery leaves and near-blue plumes. These were underplanted with cushions of the blue-grey-leaved *Hebe pinguifolia pagei*, which completely covered the ground. In summer, these are massed with tiny sprigs of white flowers. The low-growing *H. Carl Teschner* with minute green leaves and violet blossoms would serve as well, and spring colour could be added by planting some of the small bulbs, such as Chionodoxa or Scilla. Many schemes like this will suggest themselves where space is restricted.

Most seaside gardeners have an urge to plant at least one hydrangea, but owners of small gardens know that the large opulent ones often seen by the sea are not for them. One that is smaller in all its parts and would not require pruning to fit it into the garden plan, is *H. serrata acuminata*, compact and bushy, with bronzed leaves and small, white, lacecap flowers with blue central discs where the soil is acid, or pink where it contains lime. This little shrub needs plenty of moisture when coming into flower and does best if given some shade. Fuchsias and hydrangeas seem to go together in seaside gardens. They flower at the same time and are most useful for bringing late summer colour into the garden. No garden plot is too miniscule to contain the minute 'Tom Thumb' in mauve and red, and even if frost should cut the top growth it will come again from the roots.

Forsythias are probably the best known spring-flowering shrubs, providing a brilliant display of yellow flowers. Less familiar than the often planted *F. intermedia, F. spectabile*, or 'Lynwood', is 'Arnold's Dwarf', which grows slowly to a mere 2ft after some years. It flowers every bit as generously as its more vigorous relations.

SWEET PEAS FOR SEASIDE GARDENS

Strong gales blowing over gardens by the sea prevent us from growing the tall 'Galaxy' strain of sweet peas with long stems and six or seven flowers per stem, which are the joy of flower arrangers. At the other end of the scale are the 'Bijous', which have never really taken on though they have been with us for quite some time. In between were the so-called 'Knee-Hi' type. I say so-called advisedly, because whatever their height in their native California, 3ft is usual in this country. We have had great success with planting these at intervals along a lath-fencing screen that forms one of the boundaries of our garden. Here they flowered magnificently, thrusting their stems through the fence towards the sea, so that the fence became a mass of bloom and was greatly admired by passers-by. Now there is an improved type of Knee-Hi Sweet Pea, called the New Californian Strain, from the same firm which raised the original Knee-Hi strain. These grow about 3ft high and only require the support of short sticks or netting. They have larger and more brightly coloured flowers than the Knee-Hi and produce plenty of fours and fives on long firm stems. They are capable of flowering all summer if given a fairly rich soil and plenty of water during their long life. If farmyard manure is hard to come by, then garden compost with bonemeal may be used instead, or a layer of peat, spread on to the soil in which the sweet peas will be grown and mixed with a couple of handfuls of 'Growmore' per 4yd run, is excellent. The Californian Strain may be obtained in separate colours or in a mixture. Seed may be sown in a cold frame in autumn or in the open ground. The greatest menace is mice.

PLANT A MINI BORDER ON TOP OF A WALL

It is not always recognised that in gardens close to the sea there is a position on the *top* of a wall on which low-growing plants, preferably no more than 9in high, may be successfully grown. The air leaps up and over the wall, allowing small ground-huggers to flourish in what would seem an impossible situation. It is almost the last place to which newcomers to seaside gardening are likely to consider entrusting their minute plants. Yet here is a place in which plants such as gazanias, mesembryanthemums and very many so-called alpines or rock plants will do very well indeed. And if the surface of the soil is thinly mulched with grit then the chance of their survival is very high. It should be stressed, however, that they must be looked for among the real midgets, nothing soft or floppy will survive.

This kind of eye-level gardening is much appreciated by the elderly since no stooping is involved, though the fascination of these miniscule plants is not confined to those getting on in years. Children adore them.

Yet another position which is surprisingly free from the fury of the wind is the few inches immediately above the ground on the sea side of a wall or fence. This comparatively calm area of low pressure, not more than a few inches high, can be successfully exploited by the seaside gardener. Here he may safely plant his invaluable miniatures, dwarf hardy annuals, half-hardy ones or small perennial plants.

I have known annuals make a wonderfully colourful display in positions such as these. Rule out any that are too tall and make a selection from the really dwarf kinds at our disposal. The hardy annuals may be sown *in situ* in March or April. I do not advise autumn planting here, as winter gales will be too destructive for the young plants. The soil should not be on the rich side, as the object is to produce flower rather than foliage. The ground should be well-drained and well-cultivated and the seedlings should be thinned out at an early age, since it is important that each plant should be grown as tough and strong as possible. Weak specimens will not survive. Twiggy brushwood, such as the tops of the common fuchsia, is ideal for putting in among the plants while they are getting their roots down. This may look a little unsightly for a few weeks but the plants will soon cover it. Half-hardy annuals may go out in late May or early June. Keep them well watered until they are established and avoid all small plants that have become starved in their boxes.

Annuals
Alyssum maritimum Violet Queen
Anagallis
Convolvulus tricolor Royal Marine
Iberis Dwarf Fairy (Candytuft)
Limanthes douglasii
Linaria Fairy Bouquet
Matthiola bicornis (Night-scented Stock)
Phacelia
Saponaria
Silene

Half-Hardy Annuals
Ageratum Blue Blazer
Antirrhinum majus Floral Carpet
Lobelia erinus Cambridge Blue
Lobelia erinus Mrs Clibran Improved
Lobelia erinus Rosamund
Mesembryanthemum criniflorum (dorotheanthus criniflorum)
Petunia
Phlox drummondii
Portulaca
Nemesia
Tagetes Red Brocade (Marigold)
Tagetes Spanish Brocade

Minute Perennial Plants
Aethionema Warley Rose
Ajuga reptans variegata
Alyssum montanum Mountain Gold
Anaphalis margaritacea
Arabis alpina rosea
Armeria (Sea Pink)
Aubrieta
Campanula muralis
Dianthus Bombardier
Dianthus deltoides Brilliant
Dianthus Little Jock
Dianthus neglectus
Erigeron Four Winds
Euphorbia cyparissias
Gazania splendens
Geranium sanguineum
Geranium lancastriense
Helianthemum
Hypericum polyphyllum

Mesembryanthemum (*Lampranthus roseus, L. emarginatus,*
   L. aurantiacus)
Phlox douglasii
Phlox subulata
Polygonum affine
Polygonum affine Darjeeling Red
Saponaria rubra compacta
Saxifrage
Sedum acre
Sempervivum (Houseleek)
Sisyrinchium bermudianum
Solidago Queenie
Veronica prostrata

Grey-Leaved Plants for the Mini Border
Alyssum
Anaphalis
Artemisia bellidiodes
Artemisia schmidtii nana
Chrysanthemum haradjanii
Dianthus
Hebe pinguifolia pagei
Helianthemum
Helichrysum milfordiae
Potentilla beesii
Santolina incana Weston
Stachys lanata Silver Carpet (non-flowering)

Dwarf Biennials
Bellis montrosa (Double Daisy) Rob Roy, Dresden China
Dianthus barbatus Dwarf Red Monarch (Sweet William)
Myosotis Blue Ball (Forget-me-not)
Myosotis Carmine King

THE MINIATURE BULBS

The top of a wall and flat ground are both ideal places for
the small bulbs, and these are a joy to the impatient gardener.
Plant them in independent pockets or along the edge of the
mini-border, giving them as much light and room as possible.
Except in a few cases, do not plant them in the hope they will
come through other plants. They may do so for the first year
but after that their flowering will diminish. If, however, you
cannot put up with the soil left bare in summer after they
have flowered, plant them only under such creeping plants
as the alpine phloxes or the little *Geranium lancastriense* where
the sun can reach them. Avoid such encroachers as the grape
hyacinths (*muscari*), for these multiply rapidly and soon take
up more than their fair share of room. Plant instead the wee
scillas, chionodoxa, brodiaeas, chinoscillas or puschkinias. Most
scillas will seed themselves but though the more expensive
S. sibirica does not seed it makes up for it by long flowering.

SHORT PERENNIALS FOR THE SMALL GARDEN

Though for the mini-border or on top of a wall only the
real midgets should be grown, there is room in most seaside
gardens for plants of middling height that do not require
staking. Staking is useless in gardens by the sea where winds
play havoc with plant and tie, but nowhere is close planting
more necessary than with hardy perennials. They may form
part of a mixed border in which the woody structure of the
shrubs is very helpful, or they may be planted on their own in
island beds. Plants that will stand without support in an open
bed will be drawn and spindly in one beside a hedge or beneath
trees, and if excessive height is a disability in small gardens it
is an added risk in those over which the sea winds blow.

It is fatal to expose tall delphiniums, hollow-stalked lupins or 5ft Michaelmas daisies to searching sea winds, though there are a host of hardy perennial plants of medium height which do not get flattened by the first violent gale. Good, hardy plants for seaside planting will include dimorphothecas, erigerons, geraniums (cranesbills), echinops, eryngiums, kniphofias, limoniums (sea lavenders), sedums, mesembryanthemums and armerias (sea pinks). Only the middle-height members of these families will serve.

The kniphofias, or red-hot pokers, are an outstanding example of what I mean. Many of these perfectly splendid seaside plants in time achieve quite massive proportions and are out of place in a very small garden. Instead, we can plant a charming dwarf species, *K. galpinii*, with 2ft spikes of deep orange-flame and narrow, grassy leaves. It is not as frost-hardy as some others but is hardy enough for all except the coldest coasts. 'Little Goldelse' is another dwarf, with golden torches on slender, rigid stems. These look well among other perennial plants, as does the little *K. macowanii* with its rich orange pokes.

Many modern erigerons, with names mostly ending in 'ity' attract us by their very beautiful colours, though their value for seaside gardens is diminished in some cases by their somewhat lax stems that do not stand the wind. The common *E. glaucus*, pink or lilac, may not be as lovely as these other attractive varieties but it is a useful coverer for dry banks at the sea's edge, where its thickish green leaves and short daisy flowers are remarkably salt-tolerant. It is the Beach Aster of the Californian coast.

I admit to trying out the best of the tall Shasta Daisies in our windy garden, though each succeeding year they cry out for supporting stakes, without which the gales play havoc with their tall stems. A few years ago there appeared a new dwarf, compact form of *Chrysanthemum maximum,* 'Little Silver

Princess', which is extremely neat and free-flowering and useful for small windy gardens. It is easily raised from seed.

Somehow one always associates echinops and eryngium with sandy foreshore gardens, where they provide that steely-blue which is so welcome late in the season. Two good ones of only middling height are Echinops 'Veitch's Dwarf' and *Eryngium alpinum*. I have never liked the echinops or the eryngium lumped in with other herbaceous plants. They are, in fact, excellent examples of the type of plants that possess a beauty of their own, with blue flowers, stems and bracts, and are worthy of positions in which the whole plant may be admired, instead of crowded among other plants. When grown as single specimens they rarely fail to excite admiration.

Othonnopsis cheirifolia is a plant of considerable character with its fleshy glaucous leaves splaying out from either side of an ascending stem and has many possibilities in the small garden. Like most Mediterranean plants, it prefers a warm situation and a sharply-drained soil, and though it is not altogether hardy it does well in many widely varied coastal districts. The small yellow flowers are of no importance but the effective blue-green foliage persists throughout the year. To my mind, there is nothing suggesting the wallflower or, for that matter, any other member of the cheiranthus family and I have yet to discover the reason for the 'cheirifolia'. It resembles rather one of the sedums, those storehouses of water in drought conditions, and whose succulent leaves are attractive long before the flat heads of flower are colouring up in late summer. The flowers of *Sedum spectabile* are rosy-purple but are far surpassed, in my opinion, by the long-lasting flowers of 'Autumn Joy' with flowers of rosy-salmon deepening in colour as days get shorter. But the butterflies which throng the sedums vastly prefer *S. spectabile* and leave our 'Autumn Joy' alone.

There is scarcely a member of the mallow family that is not a good seaside plant, but Malva 'Primley Blue' is unusual both for its open blue mallow flowers and for the fact these are carried on long arms that keep low along the ground. I have seen and admired large plantings of the tall bearded irises in large seaside gardens, but for the pocket-sized garden there is the miniature *I. pumila* and *I. chamaeiris*. I have grown these dwarf bearded irises in pockets in paving or on top of a low wall with delightful effect. Their charming, perfectly formed flowers on short stems resemble the more familiar tall flag irises, but they are ideal small plants for the small garden. They are sun-lovers and lime-lovers and should be planted so that the tops of the rhizomes are exposed to the sun, and are best divided and replanted immediately after flowering. They flower in April and May or even in March in our garden, long before the tall flags are thinking of colouring up. They range in height from about 6 to 12in and they come in blue, yellow, purple or white. And in some of the fine new American hybrids, there are beautiful self colours as well as subtle shadings with contrasting beards. And so, for the small garden, little things are best, miniatures in their own right, small shrubs that do not need mutilation to keep them within bounds and perennial plants that do not carry too much sail to catch the winds.

9

EUCALYPTUS AND PITTOSPORUM

WHAT can it be about a eucalyptus that makes it such a status symbol in our gardens in Britain? For I am often asked by seaside gardeners what chance of success they would have with one of these beautiful evergreen trees. I find a certain gratification, tinged with amusement, among visitors to this country from 'down-under' at the interest we display in their 'gums' and in our desire to grow them. You will have other plants more worthy of attention, certainly more difficult to grow, but time and again it is the eucalyptus that steals the show. Can it be, with everyone in such a hurry these days, that it is known there is no faster-growing tree? Whatever the reason, you need one of these uniquely beautiful evergreen trees if you are to keep up with the Joneses.

The word eucalyptus, derived from *eu*=well and *kalyptos*= covered, refers to the lid on the flower bud, which keeps the flower well covered till it appears. The peculiarly lidded flower buds then fall away to reveal miniature fountains of creamy-white stamens much loved by bees. Though not all eucalyptus flowers are white; *E. ficifolia*, that grows at Tresco in the Isles

126

of Scilly, is well called the Scarlet Gum, for in a good form
the flowers are a dazzling vermilion. But this is a tender species
and doubtfully hardy even in the far south-west.

The first question we seaside gardeners have to ask ourselves
is 'Can we give the eucalypts the conditions they demand?'
We know they will stand drought, as they must do for long
periods in Australia, and many have endured quite hard frosts
in India, while in Southern Europe they flourish in spite of
driving rain. But will they tolerate sea wind round our coasts
in this country? Mr Arnold Forster used to point to the graceful *E. coccifera* growing happily enough in his garden high
up on a Cornish moor, 600ft. above sea level and exposed to
violent on-shore winds. Coming from the mountain tops of
Tasmania this is one of the hardier ones. But my own experience is that to grow the eucalypts really well in coastal
gardens they must have protection from salt-laden gales. They
will grow well at the edge of woodland, or within the shelter
of other trees, but they are not trees for full coastal exposure.
But many a garden by the sea can provide the right conditions and if not woodland, at least a tree or two to temper
the wind is what they like. In our garden where gales are
frequent and severe, *E. Gunii* has grown and flowered well,
while *E. niphophila* has survived sharp frost, heavy snow and
biting north-easterly winds without protection but was not
happy until warm spring days came again. The rather tender
E. Globulus, after a similarly hard winter, appeared completely moribund. Every leaf fell to the ground until only bare
trunk and branches remained. But after a severe pruning and
shortening of its leader, it made a truly remarkable recovery
as the sun renewed its warmth, every branch and the bare
trunk sending out new and healthy shoots and blue-green
leaves. I have had no personal experience of *E. deligatensis*
(syn. *E. gigantea*), but it is one of the hardier species and
should be worth trying in this country.

Gardens on the west coast of Scotland and in Ireland boast some of our largest trees. *E. urnigera*, which closely resembles *E. Gunnii* but has leaves of light green instead of greyish-blue, makes immense trees which flower and seed themselves. But with careful siting many hardier kinds are grown away from the milder coasts, in Essex and Kent as well as in the south-west.

The survival of many species in various parts of Britain, after the exceptionally severe winter of 1963, indicates that they may be grown in this country, but world-wide research has shown that the plant with the best chance of survival and the most rapid growth is a seedling not more than four months old from germination and no higher than 18in. It should be grown in a pot other than a clay one, to avoid root disturbance when planting out, and planted in the open ground in summer before the end of July. Unfortunately, nurserymen tell me they have found it virtually impossible to sell *small* seedlings, with the result that plants well-established in their pots, often six months old or more, are offered for sale, and these the gardening public ask for from autumn till early spring. Juvenile plants of eucalyptus with their beautiful young foliage are indeed attractive but visitors to garden centres, where they are on sale, should enquire their age and reject these enticing, well-established plants in large containers. Invariably they will have coiled roots, and even if they survive their chance of becoming beautiful trees is doubtful.

I feel we owe a debt of gratitude to Mr Richard Barnard, whose experience with the eucalyptus here and in Australia has drawn attention in this country to the reasons why these desirable trees had the reputation of being difficult.

To re-cap : for their successful establishment, all eucalypts should be planted in their final quarters when young and small, and be raised and planted from expendable pots to prevent the root disturbance they detest. They should be well

Page 129: (*above*) *Cordyline australis* in full exposure; (*below*) *Phormium tenax*, the New Zealand Flax

Page 130: *(left) Eucalyptus globulus* pruned after frost; *(right)* the same tree three months later

watered in and they should be given *maximum* light. It is likely that most Australian plants would have greater success in Britain if gardeners realised the importance that light has upon their growth.

The cheapest way to experiment with the eucalyptus is to sow seed. A great variety of these is included in Thompson & Morgan's excellent catalogue, but I suggust you try only a few of the hardiest ones as they germinate like mustard and cress. Seed of eucalyptus should be baked or soaked beforehand and my greatest success has been with seed sown in a cool greenhouse whose winter temperature did not fall below 45 degrees. Seed was sown in August, one seed to a small peat pot, but spring sowing is quicker and from seed that germinated in March I have had seedlings reach 3 to 4ft by the following August in the open ground. This 'instant' gardening has great appeal for children who cannot wait to see their plants grow.

Though their raising from seed presents no difficulty, it must be stressed that the eucalypts are not plants to be left to their own devices. They need support in their early years and certainly at first they are better for regular pruning each spring, pinching out the main stem and controlling long side branches.

Pruning

Cutting out the main leader and shortening the branches in spring provides the most beautiful foliage for indoor decoration, which will last for quite three weeks in water. It also has the effect of renewing the juvenile leaves which many people find more attractive than the adult ones. It is a remarkable feature of the eucalyptus that the same tree can produce such curiously different leaves according to its age. The young leaves may not only vary in shape, being delightfully rounded, but they stand out horizontally, while the leaves of older trees are long and tapering, hanging down like the fingers of a hand.

H

They may also vary in colour. The juvenile foliage is often a bright, glaucous blue which changes with age to an altogether staider greyish-green.

The bark of the eucalyptus is also most attractive, varying in colour with age. For, like a snake, a tree frequently sheds its skin, and since not all bark is discarded each year, the result is very lovely, a smooth mottled bark of varying colours.

Winter damage

Even if frost or gales have badly damaged the eucalypts there is still hope. Most are equipped with dormant buds to enable them to recover from damage or from cutting back, and such is the vigour of these trees that they can be cut to the ground and will in a short time reclothe themselves with leaves. Those grown for foliage production are regularly treated in this way. The time to carry out such an operation is in the spring when the sap is rising. And do not be impatient with a eucalypt which looks dead; its power of recovery is remarkable.

Hardiness

The main question in this country is one of hardiness, but I think that, with care, there are a number worth growing, particularly in gardens by the sea where temperatures are kinder and where they can be given some shelter from the coldest and strongest winds. And if seed can be obtained from trees that have proved hardy in Britain, ie, British trees, so much the better. The frost resistance of eucalypts depends much on the source of the seed.

The question is 'Which of these beautiful, evergreen, fast-growing trees is hardy enough to be worth trying in this country?' *E. niphophila* is probably one of the most frost-resistant and none was reported to have suffered frost damage after the abnormal 1963. My own tree, in a very exposed position, came through 12 degrees of frost in 1969 without loss. This gets its name of Snow Gum, not from its habitat in the Tasmanian mountains, but from the lovely white bloom on the stems of two- or three-year old trees. The large leathery leaves hanging down from red stems are wonderfully tolerant of wind. For a eucalyptus, it is slow-growing in its early stages. *E. pauciflora* is closely related to it, with large leathery leaves well spaced on reddened stems, and in mature trees the bark is reddish-brown and mottled with grey.

E. gunnii, the Cider Gum, is about the best known and universally planted in Britain since it is considered one of the hardiest. Its young, glaucous foliage is much in demand for foliage arrangements. *E. coccifera* is frost-hardy enough for the southern half of England and for coastal districts further north. Even in a windy garden, this species would be worth planting for the mealy whiteness of its bark. In shape, it resembles a small Silver Birch.

E. perriniana would be a prize for the small modern garden. This hardy mountain species makes a pretty, small tree with unusual but handsome, disc-like, blue-green leaves. The juvenile leaves grow in opposite pairs which completely fuse to form a circle around the stem. It is a most decorative plant for a large tub or to grace a paved area near the house, and it can be pollarded to keep the desired shape. The reddened stems, looking as though they have been threaded through the glaucous leaves, are much sought after by flower arrangers.

E. globulus, the Blue Gum, is probably the most widely distributed of any eucalyptus about the globe. It is one of the best for chalky soils and grows very fast indeed. From seed sown in March in a cool greenhouse I have had a 6ft tree in exactly a year's time. This was the tree that became a ghostly skeleton of bare trunk and branches, littering its huge scimitar leaves about the garden, during the winter of 1969 but completely refurbished itself to become as new. I do not advise it for the small garden as it is a greedy soil robber, but as a young plant it is very attractive indeed in a bedding scheme where it lends an exotic note. Or it can be grown in a large container on patio or terrace where its large blue-green foliage can be admired and its leaves bruised to emit the eucalyptus smell. There is a smaller, compact form, *E. globulus compacta*, with smaller leaves, but as it is of doubtful hardiness I regard these as expendable plants, worth trying for the fun of seeing how quickly they will make decorative plants for the summer garden. If they come through the winter unscathed, so much the happier. *E. delegatensis* (*Syn. gigantea*) is one of the hardier ones and one of the most salt tolerant. It has remained unaffected in cold winters when many so-called hardy trees and shrubs were badly scorched .

I hope that gardeners will be interested enough to try out some of these hardier species for themselves. They have so much to recommend them, beauty of leaf and branch, coloured bark and a decorative show of fuzzes when they flower. And even if there were no beauty of flower, the delicate arrangement of the glaucous leaves upon the branches and the graceful showering effect of some species are very eye-catching.

So far we have said little about the curiously distinctive eucalyptus smell. Some of us will remember it with distaste as too reminiscent of the remedy once used extensively for the common cold. But like it or not as you may, it once meant everything to one man in exile in this country during the war. In Cornwall, a charming tale is told of that remarkable man, Haile Selassie, Emperor of Ethiopia. He was wandering through a sunny Cornish garden just before the fall of Dunkirk in May 1940, among the brilliantly coloured rhododendrons and azaleas, when suddenly his face lit up and he asked for a small grey sprig of eucalyptus. '*C'est mon jardin*', he said, for the distinctive smell as he bruised a leaf reminded him of the eucalypts growing in his own garden at the palace at Addis Ababa, to which he was later thankfully to return.

PITTOSPORUMS

To Australasia we are not only indebted for their 'gums' but also for many of the pittosporums that are grown in this country, and, like the eucalypts, they are essentially plants for light, well-drained soil in the milder parts of Britain and for coastal areas. Native of New Zealand, the well-known *P. tenuifolium* is, perhaps, one of the hardier of the Australasian pittosporums, a 10ft shrub in most gardens but a tall tree in parts of Ireland and the south-west of England. It is worth a place in almost any seaside garden in Britain, provided it can be given protection from northerly and easterly winds and is planted where it will not get waterlogged in winter. On mild coasts it is surprisingly happy, will stand a good deal of sea wind though not severe frost, and it is often used to make protective green hedges. This is the plant whose pale green, shining leaves and black young shoots make it so attractive as a cut foliage shrub, with a ready sale to Covent Garden from the south-west where it is grown commercially. Fields of this pittosporum astonish visitors from the Midlands and the North.

Although this is the species most commonly grown in this country, there are now numerous others resulting from natural or intentional hybridisation. Though in the past the beautiful 'Silver Queen' was the only variegated form available, there are now several new forms that have been tried out in this country in the south-west to see if they would over-winter. Of these, *P. t. 'Saundersii'* survived the abnormally severe winter of 1963, and it could not have had a more bitter test than this. It is a compact, strong-growing, shrub, up to 8ft tall, with large, thickish leaves delightfully variegated with creamy-white margins that develop unusual shadings of pink late in the year. *P. t. 'Garnettii'* is very similar, also with unusual pink tints on the variegated leaves, but it is a daintier shrub, with smaller, daintier leaves, and though presumably as frost-hardy, since it too came through the winter of 1963 without loss, it looks more frail. The delicate foliage would be ideal for the florist trade and in its early stages it would make an attractive pot plant under glass before being planted into the open garden. This, I feel, is a good way to treat many of these pittosporums. If you get one, say, in the spring, from a nursery, it is often better not to plant it in the open right away. Let it grow on in a greenhouse, if you have one, for a year first, potted on as required, and plant it out the following spring. This will give it a better chance to establish itself.

One of the most enchanting and unusual pittosporums, to my mind, is a seedling from the popular 'Silver Queen'. This is *P. tenuifolium* 'Tresederi', and as its name suggests it was raised by Mr Neil Treseder at his nursery at Truro, in Cornwall. With us, it grows slowly but in time should make an erect bush from 6 to 8ft tall. It has very pretty leaves, crinkled and mottled with gold at the tips. It it quite distinct from other pittosporums and could be used to brighten a darkish corner. It is a pity that more nurserymen do not list it in their catalogues, when it would become better known in our gardens. I have not grown *P. t.* 'Purpureum', but it is reputed to be more tender than others and some losses were experienced in this country in 1963, though that abnormal winter scarcely seems a good yardstick for the vulnerability of plants. It originated in Australia and is now grown extensively in New Zealand, where it is grown as an ornamental shrub or for its cut foliage of a glossy purple, rather like that of a copper beech. It is one of the very few purple-leaved shrubs with persistent purple leaves and would make a welcome addition to gardens on our milder coasts.

These newer, attractive forms will give growers a wider selection of pittosporums to choose from, though unfortunately it is bound to be some time before they can be very widely distributed as most of them, unlike *P. tenuifolium*, must be propagated vegetatively and not from seed.

P. tobira has much stouter growth, is more widely branched, and has larger, highly glossy leaves. These polished leaves are much appreciated by gardeners on alkaline soil where rhododendrons cannot be grown. This pittosporum from Japan has conspicuous flower clusters, creamy-white and very sweetly scented. Though they are mainly produced during April and May it is not unusual to see them at other times. In its native Japan it is said to grow to 60ft or more, but in this country 8 to 10ft is more common with as wide a spread. Our own bush, some 14ft tall, was grown from seed brought home from Crete in a submarine during the last war, but its offspring are from cuttings, which root easily in a frame in summer. *P. tobira* does extremely well by the sea, appearing to be immune to quite a lot of salt spray. It does not object to shade, though it flowers more prolifically in the sun.

When I am asked which is the toughest of the pittosporums and the least frost-tender, then the answer is undoubtedly the hardy *P. ralphii*, which has survived many cold winters in north-east Yorkshire. This handsome shrub has repeatedly had to stand 20 degrees of frost and is outstanding as a wind-resister. With its long grey-green leaves, white underneath, and felted white stems, it is a most decorative shrub and excellent for coastal shelter. It will grow even on sand close to the sea. The tiny flowers are maroon-chocolate and are followed by rounded seed capsules. The more tender *P. crassifolium* is often confused with *P. ralphii* and is very similar in appearance, but its leaves are greener and more leathery, though its flowers are the same chocolate colour. But though so similar in appearance, it is nothing like as hardy as *P. ralphii* and is too tender for most mainland gardens except in the far south-west. This is the species that makes such fine hedges in the beautiful Isles of Scilly, where it is used extensively to protect cliff-top gardens and their flower farms. The leathery foliage and supple shoots seem immune to wind and salt. It was tested in various south-coast gardens before the last war but was wiped out by the bitter winter of 1940. Much later it was tried out by the Experimental Station at Rosewarne, in Cornwall, where trees and shrubs are tested for their hardiness in very exposed conditions, but only a few plants survived the winter of 1963 and those in a crippled condition. In our own garden, a hedge of *P. crassifolium* was killed after a week of 12 degrees of frost, though a few bushes still remain beneath a canopy of pines.

Though *P. tobira,* *P. crassifolium* and *P. ralphii* all show variegated forms in other countries I have not seen them here, but the tender *P. eugenoides variegatum* is a most attractive, small, round-headed tree that seems to like the shelter of other trees. Its light green, wavy-edged leaves are variegated with creamy-white and the little yellowish flowers are sweetly honey-scented. It is one of the most beautiful of variegated trees but is regrettably frost-tender and so only suited to the mildest localities.

10

VEGETABLES FOR THE
WINDY SEASIDE GARDEN

SO many of our vegetables come from abroad that when devaluation made those imports even dearer than before, many people decided, as we are doing, to grow more of their own. It also looks as though seedsmen, anticipating a rise in the cost of vegetables when we enter the Common Market, are trying to encourage us to grow more ourselves, so many and so good are some of the new kinds now on the market.

There are, however, all sorts of obstacles to growing good vegetables in windy coastal gardens, for they do not take any more kindly to sea winds than do our flowering plants. Many years' experience of trying to grow them in our garden by the sea allows me to pass on a few useful tips.

For many years a thick escallonia hedge provided the wind shelter on the sea side of our vegetable plot, and it was not until a bitter winter finally finished it off that it had to be removed. It is no use trying to stop the wind, and as no wall or close fencing is of any use, we replaced the hedge with a modern lath fencing with vertical laths an inch wide and with an inch-wide gap between the laths. This allows the wind to filter through on to the kitchen garden without opposing it. Not only had the escallonia hedge wasted a good deal of valuable room—it was 3ft across—but it kept out the light, and the winds, thwarted by a solid hedge, eddied about, causing a good deal of disturbance among the vegetables. As an alternative in a beach garden, a hedge of tamarisk is effective. It is cheap, since cuttings put in the ground in February usually take root, it grows fast even with its feet in sea water, and it is an efficient filter against salt.

Light, a free circulation of air, and moisture are essentials for good vegetable growing, but strong gales are one of the worst hazards. They not only cause damage to the plants themselves, twisting and tearing at the leaves and uprooting the brussels sprouts, but they also dry out the soil, and it was not until we installed a self-watering device to the kitchen garden that we really appreciated how very well vegetables will grow, even on an excessively sandy soil, if they are kept watered. PVC piping was laid along and bracketed on to the tops of small 2 × 2in stakes, which were driven into the ground at regular intervals round the vegetable plot. The piping was punctured with holes, the water system connected to the mains in the lane outside, a tap installed, and the whole kitchen garden can now be gently sprayed with water. Because our soil is an alkaline sand it needs more water than a heavy clay, but only a few gardens get sufficient rain for their needs, and this sort of artificial rain is easily installed and is a godsend to the owner-gardener.

To ensure that moisture is retained in the soil it is important to maintain the humus content at a high level. Sandy seashore gardeners should realise that the nutrients they have been adding to their soil are not all absorbed by the plants. A lot of them drain away with heavy rain, so every beach gardener needs to renew the organic matter in the soil year after year. Many light soils are found around our coasts and within their vicinity are copious supplies of seaweed for the taking. Something for nothing rarely fails to appeal, though it would perhaps be advisable to find out whether there are any local restrictions on removing seaweed from the beach. Seaweed contains most plant foods, particularly potash, nitrogen and iodine. It has a good effect on light sandy soils and greatly improves the retention of moisture, but before using it give it a good hosing down a few times, as too much salt is harmful to plants.

There are two types of proprietary seaweed, dried seaweed meal and liquid seaweed fertilisers, which give first-rate results. The dried form is best applied in winter as it is slow-acting and takes weeks to become effective. A dressing of 4oz to the square yard is sufficient, though double that quantity will revitalise the poorest soils. The liquid seaweed manures are quick-acting and best used as a foliar spray on vegetables during the growing season, or watered directly into the soil in the spring. But these are not cheap, while seaweed from the beach costs nothing.

Never burn seaweed or you will lose practically all organic matter and never leave it lying about the garden or it will get dry as old boots and be a harbourage for flies. Get it covered as soon as possible, stack it with straw or let it rot down in layers on the garden compost heap. If it has to be used direct on to the ground, it must be worked in some months before planting time and only then if the soil is naturally light and dry. Now a word about mulching. As we all know, a mulch, if it is thick enough—3in is good—suppresses weeds, and if it is applied after rain or artificial watering it helps to keep the soil moist. If it also has manurial value it feeds the plants, and worms and weather will do the work for you.

And now a word about the vegetables themselves. You may or may not like the Jerusalem artichoke, though it makes an excellent winter soup and is good fried around a roasted joint. It also makes a splendid tall windbreak, if a row of tubers, bought like seed potatoes in the spring, is planted across the vegetable plot. Planted 4in deep in a row with 15in between each tuber, the artichoke makes first-rate shelter for other vegetables. And since the tubers may be left in the ground as required, it is not a vegetable for the deep-freezer. And this brings us to an important decision on the part of every grower of his own vegetables. To deep-freeze or not to deep-freeze? If the family is a large one and it is thought that the initial outlay will be well repaid over the years by storing fruit and vegetables for winter use when they are expensive in the shops, then by all means go ahead. But I still think that one should take into account the vast quantity which needs to be grown to fill the cavernous jaws of the deep-freeze, and to realise that a great deal of time will have to be spent in slicing and packing during those precious summer months.

If you are not a freezer then you will want to plant only the choicest vegetables whose taste is unimpaired by their short travel from garden to pot. It is good policy, I think, never to grow a bad variety of anything, since it takes up the same room and requires the same amount of labour as a good one. Moreover, being close to the sea where it is always several degrees warmer than a mile or so inland, you will be able to take advantage of earlier crops. One should always be prepared to take a risk and plant a few early potatoes in March. Good, unfailing, early kinds are Duke of York and Sharpes Express, whose first tubers may be lifted during the last fortnight in June, and which store well until the maincrop is ready. This maincrop could consist of Pentland Crown, which has a very high yield and is a first-class cooker and a good keeper. I can thoroughly recommend it. We have grown it for some years with complete success.

One of the best beetroots is, I am sure, Crimson Globe, and new kinds like New Globe and Bolthardy give smallish crimson roots for summer salads. For early use we sow a stump-rooted carrot like Early Nantes or Early Market, and for maincrop

James Scarlet Intermediate. Pelleted seed helps spacing, reduces wastage of seed, and saves labour when thinning the seedlings. It also lessens the risk of carrot fly.

Peas are more difficult. Tall kinds are out. Some peas do better than others on different soils and Little Marvel is reputed to be good on clay. It is also excellent on our alkaline sand, and this is fortunate since only a dwarf pea such as this is suited to our windy garden. When choosing peas that really are dwarf but which produce good crops of large pods, look for varieties such as Little Marvel, Early Onward, Early Bird or Kelvedon Viscount which keep their heads down out of the wind. If you use cloches, and these are invaluable in very exposed seaside gardens, then Histon Mini is a good round-seeded, early pea listed by Unwins, only 12in tall but a heavy cropper with a good flavour. It may be sown in spring or autumn.

I first came across the dwarf Broad Bean, Dobie's Midget, in a very windswept northern island where it was heavily laden with beans. We have grown it ever since, and what a cropper it is.

The runner bean is surely the most prolific of all vegetables when it is kept cropping, but it was some years before we were able to grow it to our entire satisfaction. The usual arrangement of bean poles, criss-crossed and tied at the top, presents a solid target to the wind when laden with runners. And the wind rarely failed to bring the whole structure down just as the beans were cropping well. Re-erecting it was no good at all. The beans were ruined. A far more satisfactory method in a windy garden is to drive fir poles into the ground at 4ft intervals. Some people use bamboos, though I cannot recommend them as they are far too smooth and do not provide sufficient grip to prevent the beans from slipping. The fir poles, carrying their load of runners, present no target to the wind—it just blows through them. In the majority of cases, too many seeds are planted at one time and this results in a glut, but if the first pole is planted with six seeds around it, followed at fortnightly intervals by seeds around the remaining poles in strict rotation, this ensures a carefully spaced-out crop of runners until mid-October. Runner beans may be planted up to late June with every chance of success, provided the ground has been well prepared beforehand and is never allowed to dry out. Spraying over the plants in early evening produces the moist atmosphere they appreciate and offsets the drying winds so prevalent on the coast. Prolific runner beans, which are also good for showing, are Twenty One and Long as Your Arm. But long, straight runners are only harvested from plants on tall supports.

Should you wish to dispense altogether with poles—and in small urban gardens there is a strong case for this—then there is Hammond's Dwarf or a Dutch variety, Floret. These must not be confused with Dwarf French Beans. Except that they do not climb, they have all the characteristics of runners in shape and size. Each seed makes a small 18in high bush. They need no support of any kind but to encourage a dwarf habit any wandering shoots must be nipped back. A mulch of peat around the plants will keep the pods from being spattered with dirt in rough weather. With quick-growing crops like beans, peas and the cabbage family, it pays to add a little quick-acting fertiliser, such as an ounce of sulphate of ammonia or nitrate of soda to each yard of row, and lightly fork it in once the plants are growing strongly.

Though an alkaline soil denies us the pleasure of a vast number of lime-hating shrubs, the picture where vegetables are concerned is far brighter. Leeks, for instance, will not succeed on acid soils below a pH of 6·5, but they make a welcome change to endless savoys and brussels sprouts in the winter. I do not care for leeks so huge that they are often tough and sinewy. Holborn Model is a medium-sized one with a long season from December into April, but so hardy that it came through the bitter winter of 1963 unscathed. If sowings are made in early March, small seedlings will be ready for planting in June. Before planting them 9in apart in rows, shorten the roots as well as the tips of the plants, insert them in holes made by a dibber, water them in their holes and leave the rest to the weather. Leeks are excellent no-trouble vegetables for the seaside garden.

The ultimate size of the vegetables we grow is very important. Huge cabbages are not as popular as they once were, possibly because families are now smaller. Small, compact kinds fit better into the modern mini-plot and there is a tendency, I find, for nurserymen in their catalogues to recommend vegetables, and cabbages in particular, for their dwarf, compact habit. Small cabbages like Stonehead or Babyhead produce tight, solid hearts just large enough for a small family. I grew these last year and found they lasted for three months in the garden, even in hot weather, took up little room and were excellent for cooking or for shredding raw for salads. There is also Webb's Delicatesse, with small, ball-like heads without tough ribs, which is excellent as a basis for some salads.

Brussels sprouts are not easy by the sea. Tall kinds, full of sprouts, are rocked by the gales and this is one of the chief causes of 'blowing' of the sprouts. Earthing up the soil around the plants will help, but in very windy gardens it is best to grow a dwarf variety such as Early Dwarf, with New Year as a second cropper. Even these will require a bamboo to keep them steady in full exposure to onshore winds.

Saladings are one of the most important crops we can grow. Nothing from the shops is quite as crisp or flavoursome as one's own lettuce, straight from the garden to the table. In many a seaside garden sheltered from the worst winds, it is possible to grow lettuce unprotected through the winter for hearting up in the spring. Imperial and Arctic King give early pickings even if the tough outer leaves have to find their way on to the compost heap. May King or Attractie may be sown in autumn, to be covered with cloches at the end of October. For spring or summer sowing, the compact Buttercrunch is hard to beat and Little Gem is a first rate cos lettuce, not too tall.

The close spacing of vegetables in exposed gardens by the sea is very desirable. It provides foliage which covers the soil, preventing heat from reflecting from the ground and leaving few spaces for drying winds to dry out the soil. Cloches are invaluable for gardens in extreme exposure, but it is essential to see that they are properly closed at either end. Funnelling of the wind down the length of the cloches can make matters worse rather than better.

Page 147 : (*above*) Golden privet and red roses in a cottage garden; (*below*) Tamarisk in full exposure on the coast

Page 148 : Red Hot
Pokers at Boscastle
Harbour

11

FOR FOLIAGE EFFECT

LEAVES could supply all the colour a garden needs if only
we made fuller use of plants with gold or silver leaves,
or those whose foliage is red-purple or glaucous-blue.
These will make the garden attractive all the year and their
beautiful leaves are with us for so much longer than their
flowers. The value of these plants has been high-lighted for us
in recent years by the avid flower arrangers who are always
on the lookout for colourful and distinctive foliage to further
their designs. Colour combinations are plentiful, the colour
of one shrub or perennial plant being used to set off another.
Personally, I regard this sort of matchmaking as one of the
most fascinating facets of gardening. Half the fun of planting
is to study the effect one plant has upon its neighbour, for
plants, like humans, strike sparks off one another or remain
dumb and uninteresting.

Green and gold are always pleasing. No trouble here at all,
since there are many shades of green and I do not know one
that does not associate well with gold, to the benefit of each.
A golden-leafed shrub is quite as colourful as a plant with
yellow flowers. The Golden Privet makes a splendid splash
of bright colour. *Sambucus racemosa plumosa aurea*, the Cut

Leaf Elder, has the most beautiful, finely-cut golden leaves if pruned in early spring.

While no seaside garden worth the name is without its quota of silver plants, since these grow well in spite of wind and salt, those whose foliage is purple are none too common and have to be sought out. Purple and silver make a striking picture. Dark purple-leaved *Berberis thunbergii atropurpurea* 'Superba', with its stiff habit and large leaves, needs the lightness of a plant like *Artemisia absinthium* Lambrook Silver, whose mimosa-like spikes in summer are succeeded by silver, carrot-shaped leaves that cascade from a woody stem and persist all winter. Grey and silver lighten a garden with a frosty sparkle, particularly in dull, drear, winter days, gold and yellow simulate sunshine, the purples give richness, but a touch of glaucous-blue—and it can only be a touch, since plants with blue leaves are very few and far between—will lift a garden right out of the ordinary.

The young rounded leaves of *Eucalyptus gunnii* are very distinct, and to keep their beautiful glaucous blue one must prune it really hard in spring. The elegant shimmering leaves are greatly enhanced by a neat bush of the slow-growing *Lonicera nitida* Baggeson's Gold planted nearby, with its tiny golden leaves. This can be trimmed to make a small specimen bush or left as an informal one. Almost the best of blue foliage plants is, of course, the blue rue, *Ruta graveolens* Jackman's Blue, and to keep a good shape it pays to prune it drastically in the spring. I also cut off the yellow flowers in summer as it is so lovely grown for its blue foliage alone. It is particularly striking if planted under the golden, heath-like *Olearia solandrii*, or against a golden Cassinia.

Variations of texture can be as telling as colour associations. The spiky bronze-purple leaves of *Phormium tenax purpureum* will look twice as effective against a carpet of the soft woolly leaves of the non-flowering *Stachys lanata*. Shapes are important too. Rounded hummocks of feathery santolinas gain in beauty against the sculptured, leathery leaves of *Senecio rotundifolius*. This last is a tall, large-leaved shrub of great architectural beauty, which flourishes in extreme coastal exposure, keeping its close rounded shape in the face of wind and salt.

When planting for foliage effect, it is best to place the evergreens in prominent positions where they can be most admired and plants that lose their leaves in less conspicuous places. The same applies to tender plants, many of which are very good indeed in seaside gardens and must not be omitted altogether.

RECOMMENDED PLANTS WITH COLOURFUL FOLIAGE

The following lists of foliage plants are divided into colour groups to include trees, shrubs and hardy perennial plants. Since autumn colour is rare in seaside gardens because gales take the leaves before they have a chance to turn colour, many of those best known for changing colour at this season of the year have not been included.

Gold and Yellow

Calluna vulgaris varieties with golden foliage. 'Gold Haze' has bright golden foliage with sprays of white flowers in late summer. 'Ruth Sparkes' is a double white heather in summer with light gold foliage. 'Underwood's Variety Rosalind' has an upright habit, pink flowers in summer and brilliant golden foliage. None of these heathers is lime-tolerant.

Cassinia fulvida. A hardy shrub of heath-like effect with tiny leaves burnished with gold. It should be cut back in spring to keep it shapely.

Cupressus macrocarpa 'Goldcrest'. A golden pillar cypress of dense foliage of the brightest gold. Plant in full sun.

Cupressus mac. lutea. By far the most salt-tolerant tree for coastal planting. Rather scarce, as it is not the easiest to propagate.

Erica carnea aurea. The only winter-flowering heath with golden foliage. Bright gold in spring and early summer, with pink flowers in winter. Grows well on a limy soil. *Erica cinerea* varieties. 'Golden Drop' is a 6in heather with golden copper foliage throughout the summer. It seldom flowers. 'Golden Hue' is an 18in tall heather with light gold foliage which turns a reddish shade in winter. These need an acid soil.

Ligustrum ovalifolium aureo-marginatum. Golden Privet. Slower growing than the green form. Any green shoots should be cut out. Will not stand full exposure, but is a golden bush in shelter from the worst winds.

Lonicera nitida 'Baggeon's Gold'. Unlike the green form, it grows slowly, making a small specimen shrub of tiny yellow leaves.

Milium effusum aureum, Mr Bowles' Grass. A dwarf golden grass that can be seen in Mr Bowles' Memorial Garden at the RHS Gardens at Wisley, in Surrey. A golden form of our native millet noticed and cultivated by Mr Bowles.

Origanum vulgare aureum. The golden marjoram likes warm, light soil and full sun.

Philadelphus coronarius aureus. The golden Mock Orange is bright gold early in the season but its leaves tend to become greener as summer advances.

Rosa rugosa. In November, the veined leaves of 'Roseraie de l'Hay' and 'Blanc double de Coubert' turn a brilliant gold. All the rugosas thrive close to the sea, north as well as south.

Sambucus racemosa plumosa aurea. Some things remembered from childhood prove disappointing through adult eyes but not the Golden Cut Leaf Elder, a slow-growing shrub with very ornamental golden leaves if pruned hard in spring. Needs shelter from cold winds.

Valeriana phu aurea. A hardy perennial plant with dazzling gold leaves at the beginning of the season, darkening to green in summer. Has poorish white flowers. Is grown entirely for its golden leaves.

Silver and White

In nature, most plants with white or silver leaves come from open arid positions. Few tolerate shade or badly drained soil. Dry spots should be reserved for the silvers. Their leaves are, of course, actually green and this can be seen during and after a shower of rain. It is the tiny hairs on the leaf surfaces that give the white or silver look. The leaves of plants grown by the sea are always well covered with hairs and this leads us to believe that the hairs serve as a protection against salt spray as well as against the sun. Undoubtedly the silvers are some of the best plants we can grow by the sea.

Achillea Moonshine. A hardy perennial plant with ferny, grey leaves that persist all winter when the flat, gold flower-heads are gone.

Amelanchier villosa. A small tree, up to 8ft, with silver foliage and white flowers in spring. Grows on any soil.

Anaphalis triplinervis. A hardy perennial, seldom more than 14in tall but covers about 18in of space. The grey leaves are covered with pearly 'immortelle' flowers from July onwards.

Anthemis cupaniana. More grey than silver, the finely-cut leaves are surmounted by white daisies in early summer. The pretty foliage persists all winter.

Artemisia absinthium Lambrook Silver. A big mound of frothy grey foliage. *A schmidtii nana* makes a silky grey mound and often turns russet red in winter. Leave the dead foliage on the plant to give the young shoots protection in winter.

A. stelleriana. One of the best white-leafed plants for clay or sand, the leaf of this prostrate plant resembles that of the chrysanthemum. If staked and stopped when young as though it were a chrysanthemum, it will grow into a handsome bush like *Senecio cineraria.*

Atriplex halimus. (Sea Purslane) A wide spreading shrub of grey satiny leaves, grows rapidly on the coast. Stands full exposure.

Ballota pseudodictamnus. A soft, grey bushlet of woolly leaves.

Buddleia fallowiana Lochinch. A more compact buddleia than the type, with silver-grey foliage that persists all winter if branches are shortened in the autumn, and near-blue flowers.

Calocephalus brownii (Leucophyta brownii). A tender plant of wiry, twiggy, silver leaves. Not often seen in gardens.

Centaurea gymnocarpa. A dwarf mound of deeply-indented silvery foliage. Often used as a bedding plant, but perennial in many gardens by the sea.

Chrysanthemum haradjanii (Tanacetum densum). A dense 6in high mat of very fine silver filigree leaves. *C. poterifolium* has whiter feathery leaves.

Convolvulus cneorum. One of the most perfect small silver shrubs for seaside planting. Good even in extreme coastal exposure, particularly on sand. A star plant.

Elaeagnus argentea (E. commutata). A slow-growing, suckering shrub with rounded silver leaves.

Euryops evansii. This neat, rounded shrublet from Basutoland has intense silvery leaves that form a perfect contrast for its yellow daisies. Hardier than is generally supposed.

Helichrysum angustifolium. One of the Curry Bushes, dwarf and compact with narrow, grey leaves and small, mustard-yellow flowers on slender stems. *H. petiolatum.* A tender plant of lovely, heart-shaped, velvety silver leaves on long shoots. It is the one worthwhile bedding silver for it roots easily from cuttings, grows very fast indeed and will spread its long shoots over bare ground or up a shrub in a very short time. It is also good in urns and tubs. *H. plicatum* is a much larger edition of *H. angustifolium.* A symphony of silver and gold in summer, when a large bush is covered with long slender stems of yellow flowers but a frosty grey in winter when these have been cut off.

Hippophae rhamnoides. The Sea Buckthorn is a tall, deciduous shrub of grey, willow-like leaves and orange berries in autumn when a male is planted to windward of the females. Splendid windbreak for exposed coastal gardens, where it helps to bind the sand with its suckering shoots. Will grow with its toes in sea water.

Lavandula. The lavenders prefer a hot, dry soil and full sun. They are excellent seaside shrubs. *L. spica* is the old English lavender flowering in late summer and well into the autumn. *L. atropurpurea nana* (Hidcote) is the dwarfest form with intensely purple spikes. *L. nana* 'Munstead Dwarf' is a compact, dark-flowered variety. These last two flower early in the summer.

Olearia mollis. A small, compact, silver shrub of stiff, toothed leaves and white daisy flowers.

Onopordon acanthium. I do not know why it is often called the Scotch Thistle, since it is rare in Scotland. Its name of Cotton Thistle has more meaning, since the whole plant is covered with white, cottony-down stems, large spined leaves and small mauve thistle heads. It grows up to 6ft tall, with branching candelabra stems and will appear year after year once you have it in your garden. It is at its best against a dark background and should it seed itself in awkward places I like to remove the seedlings to a better place as soon as possible. One year, three plants appeared in a rhubarb bed which they took over, to the dislike of the rhubarb plants.

Perowskia atriplicifolia. The Afghan Sage, whose grey-feathered foliage on erect white stems and violet-blue flowers late in the summer make this hardy perennial plant a welcome addition to the late summer border. Likes full sun and dry soil and should be cut hard back each spring.

Phlomis fruticosa. The Jerusalem Sage. The large, soft-grey leaves are rather like a rabbit's ears and the strange whorls of lemon-yellow flowers are borne erect. Flower stalks should be removed as soon as the flowers are over and there will remain a lovely bush of greyish-green for the rest of the year.

Phlomis italica. The leaves are just as furry as those of the Jerusalem Sage but whiter, and the flowers the palest pink, clustered in tiers on erect, branching stems. It comes from the Balearic Islands and is not as tough as *P. fruticosa.*

Potentilla mandschurica. A dense, prostrate bush of small grey leaves and white, saucer flowers.

Potentilla vilmoriniana. A tall, erect shrub of silver-grey leaves and cream flowers. All shrubby potentillas may be pruned hard in spring and are excellent for coastal gardens in the north and east where they have a very long flowering season.

Salvia argentea. One of the most exciting of the silvery biennials. A plant from Southern Europe, which mostly dies after flowering once, but do not allow it to put on its pale, pinkish-white flowers and it can be kept alive for years. In any case the flowers are of no value, but the large, flat tufts of leaves, coated with soft, silky hairs, are very handsome. Plant it in light, well-drained soil and surround it with some snail deterrent.

Santolina chamaecyparissus. (S. incana) The Lavender Cotton, or French Lavender. A beautiful hummock of frosty grey and profusions of gold, button flowers in summer. If a bush is severely pruned in March a bush will preserve its foliage effect all summer; if pruned over after summer flowering it will flower again the following year.

Santolina neapolitana. A much taller shrub of very finely cut feathery silver foliage. *S. incana* 'Weston' is a very small santolina, never more than 10in high, white and woolly. All santolinas are excellent for dry walls in full exposure.

Senecio cineraria. (Cineraria maritima). Often used as a bedding plant but is perennial on many coasts where it grows wild. Better garden forms are 'Ramparts' with silver leaves, and 'White Diamond' with oaklike leaves which are startlingly white. Cut back in early May. A newer form which I have grown from seed is 'Silver Dust', a shorter plant with deeply-indented grey leaves, good for the front of a border. I discovered *S. c. candicans*, often listed as *Cineraria candicans*, in the Connaught Gardens at Sidmouth, where it made an attractive pewter-grey edging of broad leaves. I have only seen it once before and this was at Tenby in Wales. It is easily propagated from seed and this is the best way to obtain this rather uncommon but worthwhile plant. *S. laxifolius* is a 'must' for coastal planting, one of the toughest and most decorative large shrubs, with clear-cut grey leaves with white undersides and white stems. There is no need to hack it about if it is groomed from infancy. It is questionable whether a shrub in a prominent position should be allowed to flower and the leaves deteriorate as soon as the yellow daisies begin to set seed. *S. l. compacta* is better for small gardens.

S. leucostachys is a tender plant of lacy, silver-white leaves on long stems, that is worth keeping going from cuttings. It needs a starvation diet to produce its best colour. It likes to thread its way through the bare branches of another shrub, or climb among herbaceous plants where its legginess can be concealed.

Stachys lanata (Lamb's Tongue) makes a dense, woolly carpet of soft grey leaves topped with soft lavender flowers with felted stems. The newer, non-flowering variety, 'Silver Carpet' is a better ground coverer.

Teucrium fruticans. A fast-growing shrub of pale grey leaves, white stems and pale lavender flowers. It is very wind-tolerant.

Zauschneria californica. A dwarf perennial plant for dry soils, of grey, feather-like foliage and bright scarlet, tubular flowers in late summer.

Red-Purple and Bronze

Ajuga reptans atropurpurea. An invasive small carpeter with rich bronze-purple leaves, that can be used with good effect to underplant grey-leafed shrubs, where its spreading habit is what is required.

Berberis thunbergii atropurpurea. A 4 to 5ft shrub of small, red-purple leaves through spring and summer. Makes a good hedge.

Berberis t. a. nana has foliage as the previous variety but is a slow-growing dwarf form, excellent as a foil for gold or silver plants.

Berberis t. a. 'Superba'. Has larger, deep purple leaves and in time makes a tall, upstanding bush of great beauty.

Cotinus coggygria Notcutt's Variety. (*Rhus cot. Foliis Purpureis*). The Smoke Tree, so called because of the smoky-grey inflorescences. The dark maroon foliage of this superb variety never loses its freshness, a wonderful colour that never fails to attract attention and is splendid in association with other plants to their mutual enhancement, eg, *Cupressus macrocarpa* 'Goldcrest'.

Phormium tenax purpureum. A tender and rather rare form of the New Zealand Flax that needs more shelter from salt-laden gales. Plant it where the sun can shine through its clearcut, sword-like, bronze-purple leaves.

Pittosporum tenuifolium 'Purpureum'. One of the few shrubs whose purple leaves persist and might be called the 'everpurple'. The leaves of this tender shrub are small, dark-purple with wavy margins.

Polygonum affine. Much as I appreciate the dainty crimson flowers of 'Darjeeling Red', and the flower spikes of deep rose deepening to garnet-red of the 'Lowndes variety', in winter it is their bronze-red foliage that is so valuable.

Prunus cistena 'Crimson Dwarf'. This new and very striking purple-leaved, dense shrub, about 4ft tall, is effective when planted in a group or as a small hedge inside the garden.

Salvia officinalis purpurea. This colourful sage makes a mound of soft purple foliage, bluish in cold weather and rich violet in the spring.

Vitis vinifera purpurea. This hardy climbing vine has leaves at first claret then purple.

Weigela florida 'Foliis Purpureis'. An invaluable shrub for the mixed border with purple foliage and pink flowers blending attractively. Slow-growing, it takes about four years to reach 5ft.

Scarlet
Probably the most startlingly beautiful of shrubs with brilliantly coloured leaves is *Pieris formosa* var. Forrestii, named after

George Forrest, who must have been astounded when he came
across it blazing on the slopes of its native mountains in the
province of Yunnan in China. People blink in unbelief when
confronted with this amazing tall shrub whose scarlet young
shoots in spring they mistake for flowers. Though the lily-of-
the-valley-like flowers, creamy and sweetly-scented, are most
beautiful, it is the young foliage that is the glory of the plant.
Unfortunately, it is a lime-hater and will only grow on rhododendron soil. It dislikes cold winds and must have shelter from
them; it also dislikes late spring frosts and who shall blame it?
Yet this extravaganza of a shrub may be seen in many a sheltered garden by the sea, on the west coast of Scotland, in
Ireland and in Cornwall, and if you cannot grow it because
you cannot supply its needs, you should seek it out and take
a picture of it as I have done.

Glaucous Blue

Cedrus atlantica glauca. The Blue Cedar is surely the most
beautiful of all blue-grey trees, a tree of large dimensions with
slender, horizontal branches. I could wish it grew more quickly
on our dry, sandy soil, yet I would not be without this most
impressive of all the glaucous conifers, and it can be pruned
if the garden is a small one.

Dianthus. The Pinks have very good glaucous foliage and
clumps are most attractive in the garden even when not in
flower. Sharp drainage and preferably a limy soil and a sunny
position are needed for them.

Eryngium maritimum. The wild Sea Holly has the bluest leaves
of all eryngiums but the general effect of garden forms, such
as *E. alpinum*, *E. oliverianum* and *E. planum*, is distinctly
blue. These are valuable for late summer colour.

Eucalyptus species. Very many have valuable glaucous foliage.
(See Chapter 9.)

Euphorbia myrsinites. A small, prostrate spurge with intensely blue, fleshy leaves and yellow flowers. Happiest basking on a sunny wall.

Festuca ovina glauca. Does not spread or seed itself to become a nuisance but remains a delightful, neat, little glaucous grass.

Hebe pinguifolia pagei. An excellent ground covering plant of dense mat-forming small grey-blue leaves and white flowers.

H. pinguifolia. An erect small bush of little glaucous leaves and small lavender flowers.

Helictotrichon sempervirens. This beautiful glaucous grass should be planted so that it can be viewed from all angles. As its name implies, it is good all the year and so is useful for the winter garden.

Othonnopsis cheirifolia. This doubtfully hardy plant has paddle-shaped, glaucous leaves on either side of long stems and yellow, fleshy flowers early in the year.

Ruta graveolens Jackman's Blue. Surely the bluest foliage of dwarf garden plants. The ferny foliage of the blue rue makes a lovely pool of colour. Prune it hard in the spring.

With so large a range of shrubs and perennial plants at our disposal, there is no need for the dreary bareness of beds and borders in winter where these are grown. The steely blue of lavender persists all winter, the silver leaves of *Convolvulus cneorum* have become a lovely shade of pewter with colder weather, the gilded rosemary is never more beautiful than when lit by a wintry sun, and the persistent foliage of grey-felted Phlomis makes up for the loss of its strange lemon-yellow whorls. Add to these the bergenias, known variously as saxifrage or megasea, whose bold glossy leaves have turned to shades of red or purple. The foliage of *B. delavayi* has become an attractive bright crimson, while B. 'Evening Glow' is copper-bronze. I love the contrasts of form and colour, and as I walk round my garden on some dull winter's day I am more convinced than ever that it is on foliage effect that a garden largely depends.

12

THE AUGUST GARDEN
BY THE SEA

SHOULD it be wondered why I devote an entire chapter
in a book on seaside gardening to the August garden, it
is because this is the month, above all, when the annual
surge of visitors to the sea takes place. Seaside gardens reach
their peak at high summer when public gardens at seaside
resorts put on their bravest display and small gardens are
mosaics of colour and beauty. Inland gardens are often deserted
at this holiday period and we who live by the sea have a special
responsibility to make our gardens attractive and interesting
at this time, since many of the plants we grow are unfamiliar
to inland visitors.

There was a time when August-flowering shrubs and hardy
perennial plants were the only ones of absorbing interest to
me, for I was mainly concerned with getting as much colour
as I could into our cottage garden by the sea in August. Now
that I live the year round on the coast and our garden has
to have its fair share of colour at other times, I look round the
garden in August with a critical eye to see how I can get more
colour into it, and I came to the conclusion that we must have
more hydrangeas.

One is often told that flowering shrubs are past their best by August, though on the coast this is the time when many can be in full flower, if the trouble has been taken to plant them. On the west coast, in particular, where more humid conditions suit the always thirsty hydrangeas, no flowering shrub lasts long in bloom, and in August their beautiful blues and purples where the soil is acid, or pink and red where there is lime, are the highlights of many coastal gardens. The solid, rounded heads of the mopheads are spectacular close to the house, down flights of steps or in tubs and containers, while the flattened flowerheads of the lacecaps are most beautiful in some shade. Owners of small gardens should ask the nursery-man for small varieties as heavy pruning of larger kinds restricts their flowering, and should mention the kind of soil they have, since much disappointment is often caused by buying blue varieties that turn pink or red on a soil that is highly alkaline. But this is where tubs and containers come in. Hydrangeas are excellent tub plants provided they have ample humus, peat, old manure, etc, and are never allowed to suffer from lack of water. Red varieties are best on sunny terraces, with the blues and whites against a cool, north-facing wall, and since we are unable to grow the bright blues on our limy soil, we have them instead in large tubs of specially prepared acid soil where they give a spectacular display for many months.

To my mind, one of the most satisfying of the mopheads is 'Westfalen' with chunky, globular, vivid red or purple flowers. Flowering shoots keep coming from the base rather like an herbaceous plant. Though the outstandingly beautiful sky-blue or rose-pink 'Generale Vicomtesse de Vibraye' comes early into flower, it continues at its best over a very long period. 'Mme Emile Moulliere' is pure white with no hint of pink or blue and is at its loveliest in shade. For small gardens, compact kinds such as Ami Pasquier, Vulcain, Parsifal and Preziosa are best.

The lacy lacecaps have flattened flowerheads, with an outer ring of large sterile florets and a contrasting central disk of small fertile flowers. Two popular ones are the hardy, vigorous 'Blue Wave' and its white equivalent 'White Wave', but for smaller gardens there is the long-flowering 'Lanarth White', only 2 to 3ft high with a spread of around 4ft, and 'Grays-wood', an erect bush with dainty lacecap flowers in August.

If you have more room to fill in a garden where frost is not unknown, then the very lovely *H. villosa* is the one for you. I remember Colonel Stern telling me that this was the finest August-flowering shrub he grew in his chalk garden at Highdown, near Worthing, in Sussex. It is one of the few hydrangeas that has lavender-blue flowers on a chalk or limy soil, and it stands very dry, hot conditions. It is also perfectly hardy, as the flowers are carried on the new shoots and these do not appear till the frosts are over. It comes into flower in the middle of August, covered all over with beautifully-poised, flat heads of flower, clear violet-blue at the centre with outer sterile florets of the palest lavender. But this is not all. The stems, flower stalks and under surfaces of the leaves are tawny grey and hairy, and the leaves themselves look and feel like soft green velvet. A large bush, often some 8ft high and nearly as much across, is a spectacular sight.

Should your garden lie in a 'notorious frost-pocket', then you may plant the cast-iron hardy *H. paniculata grandiflora*. It will survive the worst possible conditions. A group of young plants in a border is an unforgettable sight of enormous, cone-shaped flowers, first green, then cream, slowly turning pink with age. Do not allow it to make many branches, but prune it hard in early spring to produce a fine show of its huge flowers in August. The self-clinging *H. petiolaris*, with ethereal white lacecap flowers, is no less hardy and has other uses than the familiar one of growing against a wall. It is quite as happy

L

climbing up a tree or it makes a fine bush, if pruned, in the open garden.

Now that we know which fuchsias we can safely leave in their permanent positions in the garden to over-winter there is no need to restrict ourselves to the small-flowered *F. magellanica riccartonii*, which cannot compare in size of flower or colouring with some of the large-flowered fuchsias like Mrs Popple, Margaret, Mme Cornelissen, Lena, Rose of Castile and Tom Thumb. Their top growth may be cut to the ground in early spring like any herbaceous plant and yet be full of flower in August. Their bright colours are much enhanced by a nearby planting of the gentian-blue *Ceratostigma willmottianum*, or the soft, lavender blue of caryopteris. When one bitter winter a hedge of bright blue rosemary collapsed and died on us, we replaced it with a hedge of the tougher and lime-tolerant *Erica terminalis*, gay with pink flowers in August and the only summer-flowering erica that does well on alkaline soils.

Gardeners in mild inland gardens despise, I know, the olearias from New Zealand. They call them drab, and perhaps rightly so, for their daisy flowers in August are not truly white and soon turn a soft brown. But how well their leathery leaves and daisy flowers suit some rugged windswept coasts, battered for much of the year by constant violent gales. *O. haastii* is the hardiest, and tough enough for the cold north-east coast, where it provides protection for other plantings. *O. albida* is scarcely less hardy but taller and more showy in flower. One should be grateful for such shrubs as these. The hoherias, the New Zealand Lace-Barks, are surprisingly wind-resistant on the coast and develop quickly into tall, slender trees of honey-scented, white flowers borne in dense clusters during August. Two wind-tolerant ones are *H. glabrata*, weighed down with branches of fragrant white flowers, or the evergreen *H. sexstylosa pendula*, a weeping form with cascades of scented, white flowers. Eucryphias are mostly acid peat-lovers but a first cross, *E. 'Nymansay'*, is tolerant of some lime and is a wonderful sight in August, when this small upright tree is a mass of white, open flowers with a boss of golden anthers at the centre.

The hypericums include some of our most valuable late-flowering shrubs on any soil, and when pruned hard in spring the hardy *H. patulum* Hidcote makes a dense, rounded bush smothered with yellow saucer flowers in August. The erect 'Rowallane Hybrid' has clusters of large, deep buttercup-yellow flowers but is only evergreen in mild localities. It is one of the most beautiful of all St John's Worts where it can be grown satisfactorily. There is even a hypericum for gardens of miniscule proportions, for *H. polyphyllum* grows only a foot high, a small bushlet of tufts of erect stems bearing a multitude of scarlet-tinged buds which open to surprisingly large, yellow, saucer-flowers for so small a shrub.

Hibiscus are often disappointing, because they are grown in shady situations whereas they must have full sun to flower really well, so that they do particularly well on south or east coasts where the light is good. They are slow to come into leaf, and so miss the worst of the spring gales. Among the best are 'Blue Bird' deep blue-mauve, 'Hamabo' pale blush with a crimson basal blotch, and 'Woodbridge' dark rose-pink with a central blotch of dark maroon.

HARDY PERENNIAL PLANTS FOR THE AUGUST GARDEN

Not all hardy herbaceous perennial plants are suitable for sea-side planting, but one of the most outstanding for the August garden is the red-hot poker, or kniphofia. It stands full exposure on our coldest coasts. Kniphofias like a rich soil, one that has been well-prepared beforehand, a sunny situation and they detest bad drainage and winter wet. They dislike disturbance and should be transplated only in spring when necessary.

There are varieties for flowering from early spring until autumn, but good August-flowering ones are Mount Etna, John Benary, August Gold and Samuel's Sensation and, for very small gardens, the little 2ft *K. macowanii.*

Very dry, sandy seashore gardens are always a problem, but they can well be the place for the sea hollies. The true sea holly, *Eryngium maritimum,* is not often found today thrusting its woody roots down into a sandy beach, but good garden forms with striking, steel-blue teazles, stems and bracts are unique among perennial plants for August. *E. alpinum* is only about 18in high and not only are the oblong flowers a beautiful bright blue but spiky ruffs as well. *E. oliveranum,* the little *E. planum* and *E. amethystinum* are all to be found in gardens, giving that touch of steely blue that is so desirable in the late summer garden, but a startling and unusual species which I have included among my 'star' plants is the newer *E. proteiflorum.* This has been variously described to me as 'the most attractive and striking herbaceous plant seen for years', 'the most beautiful and unusual flower ever seen' and 'the discovery of a decade'. You should grow it and see for yourself.

Echinops, the Globe Thistles, are often closely associated with eryngiums and they like the same dry, well-drained soil, full sun, and they flower at the same time. Their thistle heads are also blue. *Echinos* = hedgehog and *ops* = like, and the round flowerheads are slightly reminiscent of a rolled-up hedgehog. They vary in height from 'Veitch's Blue', a deep bright blue, only 2ft high, to 'Taplow Blue', 5ft or more. A plant which associates very happily with the echinops is *Aster linosyris.* The blue and yellow look well together in the flower border. This is a first-rate plant for a windy seaside garden as, in the wild, it often inhabits limestone cliffs in the west of Britain. Often called 'Goldilocks', it rarely grows taller than 20in and has slim, tough stems that never need staking. Its foliage is so light as to be barely noticeable, but the individual flower-heads are rich yellow and borne in flattened terminal clusters, 3 to 5in across. Even a small plant provides a spot of eye-catching colour. Known variously in nurserymen's catalogues as *Linosyris vulgaris, Crinitaria linosyris* and *Chrysocoma linosyris,* it is the same worthwhile plant.

The sedums, the so-called ice-plants, are splendid seaside plants and wonderfully tolerant of salt winds. They also stand drought well. In August, they spread pools of colour above their fleshy glaucous foliage. *S. spectabile* has flat heads of flower of mauve-pink, the long-lasting flowers of 'Autumn Joy' start salmon-pink, later turning to coppery-rose which endures well into the autumn, and 'Brilliant', which received an Award of Merit in 1961, has large flat heads of the richest pink. Butterflies adore them.

Foliage, as we have seen, is tremendously important in a garden and should you have a key position to fill, or a strategic corner where handsome evergreen leaves and tall erect flower spikes will make wonderful garden furnishing, then you cannot do better than plant *Acanthus spinosus.* It stands both wind and drought thanks to its stout, tenacious roots which anchor it in the ground, and never requires staking. It thrives on chalk or lime but resents disturbance and is not easy to transplant so that its position, preferably but not necessarily open to the sun, needs careful siting. It has prickly, deeply divided, glossy green leaves, the young foliage is less pointed and not as deeply cut as in a mature plant and, in August, has majestic flower spikes of purple, green and white which last for a very long time. In classical times the acanthus leaf served as a motif for ornamental carving, particularly for Corinthian columns. Today, the flower spikes dry beautifully but they must be cut before the seeds are formed, otherwise the seeds shoot from their calyces when the spikes are brought into a warm room.

For a position of similar importance, but in full sun, a yucca makes an ornamental addition to any garden for its foliage alone, and provided you keep it happy with plenty of air, light and good drainage, with a soil on the light side, it will burst into bloom in great splendour, with towering spires of creamy bells most summers. *Y. filamentosa* is the one most commonly grown, since it flowers at an early age and with greater regularity than the spectacular *Y. gloriosa*. No protection whatever is needed for yuccas, they flower in extreme coastal exposure but will not thrive where static winter wet alternates with hard frost.

It is high time we seaside gardeners ceased to grow our Agapanthus Lilies—with narrow strap-like leaves and tall umbels of many open-trumpet flowers, varrying in colour from palest to deepest blue and even white—solely in large tubs and containers, bringing them in under cover for winter protection and taking them out again into sun lounges or sunny terraces as soon as the weather warms up. It is quite unnecessary, and in a number of gardens by the sea which I have visited these herbaceous perennials from South Africa are growing in great drifts on open ground. In extra mild maritime situations, such as in the Abbey Gardens at Tresco, in the Isles of Scilly, they seed themselves about the garden and even on the trunks of palm trees. In colder gardens, they may have some slight covering over their resting crowns in winter but there is increasing proof that many species beside the hardy, dark blue 'Mooreanus' require only some little protection, and now that we have the hardy 'Headbourne Hybrids' these may safely be left in the ground in colder districts on the coast. Should transplanting ever become necessary, then the plants may be split up in early spring and given some rich soil in which to start again.

One of the loveliest of late summer flowering plants of recent introduction has undoubtedly been *Crocosmia mason-*

orum, and so beautiful are its huge, monbretia-like, intense reddish-orange flowers that I have given it 'star' treatment in the August garden. Plant the corms in spring. Another August-flowering bulb from South Africa which I do not care to be without is *Galtonia candicans*. Sometimes called the Giant Summer Hyacinth, it has white, pendulous flowers tinged with green, carried on stout 4ft stems. I like them best in small groups, rising up among herbaceous plants which help to conceal their large green leaves.

And if you are fortunate enough to have a sunny, open position in a garden where frost is never severe, you will plant some of the perennial mesembryanthemums for August colour. In California, literally scores of kinds of these semi-succulent plants are used as ground cover by the sea. The common mezzie, *Carpobrotus edule* (*M. edule*), has large fleshy leaves and pink or yellow flowers and may be seen trailing down over rocky cliffs splashed with salt, but more suited to small gardens are the little 'mezzies' with smaller leaves and flowers that open to the sun in pink, violet-purple or orange-red. They go under such names as *Lampranthus roseus*, *L. emarginatus* and *L. aurantiacus*. Pieces may be pushed into a sandy soil where every bit will root. They may be grown in the crevices of walls, or right on top of a wall at the sea's edge.

Here, too, will the gazanias thrive, not simply the low spreading *G. splendens* but many of the newer, exciting hybrids of prostrate habit. These may be grown from seed in early spring to produce flowering plants for late summer. On a sunny ledge or in a crevice in a dry wall, *Zauschneria californica*, sometimes called the Californian Fuchsia because of its showy spikes of bright scarlet flowers, will give you weeks of vivid colour. It enjoys any amount of hot sun and drought but is not too hardy, so that cuttings of non-flowering shoots should be taken in a frame during early autumn.

APPENDIX

Sources of Supply for Plant Material

For shrubs, trees and hardy perennial plants
Treseder's Nurseries, Truro, Cornwall.
R. C. Notcutt, Woodbridge, Suffolk.
Toynbee's Nurseries, Bognor Regis, Sussex.
St Bridget Nurseries, Old Rydon Lane, Exeter, Devon.
George Jackman & Sons, Woking, Surrey.
Slieve Donard Nurseries, Newcastle, Co. Down, N. Ireland.
Hillier & Sons, Winchester, Hampshire.
Joe Elliot, Broadwell, Moreton-in-Marsh, Glos.
Alan Bloom, Bressingham Gardens, Diss, Norfolk.

Bulbs and corms, etc
P. de Jager & Sons, Marden, Kent.
Messrs Blom, Leavesdon, Watford, Herts.

Seeds
Thompson & Morgan, Ipswich, Suffolk.
Sutton & Sons, Reading, Berkshire.
Samuel Dobie, Chester.
Thomas Butcher, Shirley, Croydon, Surrey.
Geo Roberts, Faversham, Kent.

I receive a number of requests for rare and unusual plants. For these, write direct to The Plant-Finder Service. The Horticultural Trades Association, 6th Floor, Cereal House, Mark Lane, London, E.C.3. But do not bother them for plants in any of the above catalogues.

INDEX

173